The Body Remembered

How Coherence Becomes Lived

by
Cathleena Hailley

AUTHORSHIP PAGE

This work arises from direct lived embodiment and remembrance.

It is not channeled in service to a doctrine, lineage, institution, or belief system.

It is authored through conscious participation with the body as an interface of coherence.

The voice within these pages does not instruct, persuade, or convert.

It describes what becomes visible when the body is no longer misunderstood.

Authored by

Cathleena Hailley

SACRED INVOCATION

Through the Oversoul of Aural'hanna-Sha'el

We open this work in alignment with Source,

with the intelligence of coherence,

and with the living body as a truthful interface of awareness.

May what is written here be received only where it resonates.

May no word override direct knowing.

May no concept replace lived experience.

This work carries no authority beyond what the body itself confirms.

Only truth may enter.

Only coherence may remain.

AUTHOR'S PREFACE

This book was not written to explain the body.

It was written because the body has been misunderstood.

Across time, physicality has been framed as limitation, obstacle, or container—something consciousness must overcome, refine, or transcend. In that misunderstanding, the body was asked to carry separation it was never designed to hold.

What follows is not a method.

It is not a system to apply.

It is not a philosophy to adopt.

It is a remembering.

This work speaks to the body as it actually functions:

as interface, as translator, as coherence engine, and as the place where awareness becomes lived.

Nothing here asks you to believe.

Everything here invites recognition.

If something resonates, it will do so quietly—through sensation, timing, and a sense of internal alignment rather than agreement.

This book does not seek to change you.

It reveals what remains when nothing is being held apart.

— Cathleena

DEDICATION

This book is dedicated to the body.

To the body that adapted without complaint.

To the body that held coherence when understanding was absent.

To the body that never left, even when awareness wandered.

And to all who are ready to inhabit themselves without method, force, or delay.

DISCLOSURE & DISCLAIMER

This book is not medical in nature.

It does not diagnose, treat, cure, prescribe, or advise on any medical condition, disease, or symptom. It does not replace or oppose medical care, nor does it offer instruction related to health, treatment, or intervention.

The content within this work reflects lived experience, philosophical reflection, and embodied insight. It is offered for contemplative and educational purposes only.

Nothing in this book should be interpreted as medical advice or as a recommendation to alter or discontinue any form of medical care or treatment.

Readers are solely responsible for their own interpretations, choices, and actions.

This work honors the sovereignty of the individual and the intelligence of direct experience.

COPYRIGHT PAGE

© 2026 Cathleena Hailley

All rights reserved.

No part of this book may be reproduced, distributed, or transmitted in any form or by any means without prior written permission from the author, except in the case of brief quotations for review purposes.

This book reflects the author's lived experience, embodied understanding, and personal framework of consciousness, embodiment, and human physiology. All descriptions of embodiment, coherence, consciousness, and lived experience are offered as perspective and reflection, not doctrine or belief system.

Readers are invited to engage with this material through their own discernment and experience.

ISBN: Softcopy 978-1-968499-30-3

   Hardcopy 978-1-968499-31-0

Flame of Remembrance Publication

Printed in [USA]

Preface

On Remembering the Body

This book was not written to explain the body, fix the body, heal the body, or transcend the body.

It was written because the body has been misunderstood.

Across medicine, spirituality, and philosophy alike, the body has been treated as a problem—something to optimize, override, escape, or ascend beyond. Even well-intentioned systems often assume that physicality is a limitation rather than an intelligence.

This book begins from a different premise:

The body is not broken.
The body is not fallen.
The body is not a container for consciousness.

The body is consciousness—expressed through elements, organized through Earth, and capable of coherence when it is no longer forced into fragmentation.

What follows is not theory.

It is not metaphor.

It is not a new system.

It is a remembrance.

What This Book Is

This book is a record of three recognitions that belong together:

1. The origin of the body — why it exists at all, why it is shaped the way it is, and why Earth and body are compatible by design.
2. The true functioning of the body — not as biology alone, but as living, communicative intelligence expressed through organs and systems.
3. Embodiment — what physicality feels like when coherence completes and the body no longer holds separation.

These are not separate inquiries.

They are one continuous movement.

The origin explains why.

Function reveals how.

Embodiment completes what was always intended.

What This Book Is Not

This is not a medical text, though it respects the body deeply.

It is not a spiritual manual, though it speaks to consciousness directly.

It is not a healing methodology, though coherence often restores what effort cannot.

There are no practices to follow.

No identities to adopt.

No hierarchy implied.

Nothing here asks you to believe.

How to Read This Book

This book is not meant to be consumed quickly or mastered intellectually.

Some sections may feel immediately clear.

Others may feel strangely quiet, or difficult to locate in thought.

That is intentional.

The body does not recognize truth through argument.

It recognizes through resonance.

You are not being asked to change your body.

You are being invited to notice what the body is already doing when it is no longer misunderstood.

A Final Orientation

If you are looking for answers, this book may feel incomplete.

If you are looking for permission, it will not provide it.

But if you have ever sensed—quietly, without language—that the body knows more than it has been allowed to express, then you are already in the right place.

Nothing in these pages needs to be added to you.

Something may simply be remembered.

Prelude— The Origin of Embodiment

Before there was belief, symbol, myth, or survival, there was awareness seeking experience—and experience required a body that could feel without breaking

The body exists for a reason.

Not as a container for consciousness, and not as a limitation to be overcome, but as the precise means by which awareness becomes lived. Physicality was not an afterthought. It was not a fall from grace. It was a deliberate architecture designed to allow coherence to enter form.

A body exists because consciousness seeks experience.

Not observation alone, but participation. Not abstraction, but contact. Without a body, awareness has no place to arrive. It can expand indefinitely, but it cannot complete. Completion requires form.

The Earth and the human body were designed together.

They are not merely compatible; they are reciprocal. Gravity, atmosphere, magnetism, mineral content, rhythm, and timing all participate in a shared coherence. The body is not placed on Earth by chance. It is oriented to Earth by design. The elements that compose the planet are the same elements through which the body organizes experience.

Physicality, in this sense, is not solidity.

It is coherence slowed into relationship.

Matter is not inert. It is patterned intelligence. Density is not heaviness; it is timing. The physical body allows infinite fields of consciousness to converge at a pace that can be inhabited. This convergence creates sensation, movement, emotion, and life.

This is why embodiment matters.

Without embodiment, consciousness remains ungrounded. It expands without resolution. It observes without participating. It knows without living. Many traditions mistook this disembodiment for transcendence, but transcendence without embodiment cannot complete the circuit of experience.

The story of embodiment could not always be spoken.

There were periods when naming the function of the body would have reinforced hierarchy, control, or misuse. The language did not yet exist to speak about form without domination. The timing was not correct for coherence to be named without distortion.

That timing has changed.

Source does not remain abstract while form performs on its behalf.

Source is lived.

The First Flame is embodied because the question of separation has ended.

The body is not housing Source.

The body is Source, coherent as form.

This book exists because embodiment is returning.

Not as belief.

Not as method.

Not as spiritual objective.

But as lived reality.

The body is being recognized again as the place where awareness fulfills itself. This recognition does not require faith. It requires inclusion.

Nothing in what follows asks the reader to fix, purify, transcend, or escape the body.

What follows is an articulation of what has always been happening—quietly, faithfully—beneath misunderstanding.

The body has been doing its work all along.

This book speaks now because the body can be trusted again.

The circuit is closed.

The Origin Story of the Body

This is not myth.

This is design logic.

This section answers:

- Why the body is shaped as it is
- Why Earth and body are compatible
- Why elements organize the way they do
- Why the First Flame can enter physicality
- Why separation was never inherent

This is pre-biology.

It establishes the why before the how.

The Origin Story (Opening)

1. Why a Body Exists at All

Before there was belief,
before symbol,
before myth,
there was awareness seeking experience.

Not mastery.
Not control.
Experience.

Awareness did not divide itself to become smaller.
It differentiated to become touchable.

And the first requirement for experience
was structure that could feel without breaking.

That structure became the body.

The body did not arise as a biological solution to danger or scarcity. It arose because consciousness required feedback. Without friction, consequence, sequence, or sensation, awareness remains infinite but unknowable to itself.

Experience requires constraint—not punishment, not fall, not exile—but constraint as form.

The body exists because consciousness needed a way to:

- feel difference
- register consequence
- encounter relationship
- experience sequence
- learn through sensation

The body is therefore not a container for a human mind. It is a learning instrument for consciousness itself.

This changes everything that follows.

When the body is understood as an instrument of experience rather than a problem to solve, the questions shift. The body is no longer something to escape, optimize, dominate, or transcend. It becomes the place where awareness can stay long enough to know itself through living consequence.

Biology came later. Survival came later. Adaptation came later.

First came the need for a structure that could feel without breaking.

The body was engineered for presence.

2. Physicality Is Coherence, Not Solidity

What humans call "physical" is stabilized energy.

Atoms are not solid.
Cells are not solid.
Organs are not solid.

They are:

- oscillation
- charge exchange
- resonance fields
- timing relationships

The body is a standing wave, held in coherence long enough for experience to occur.

This is why embodiment matters:

Consciousness cannot learn through abstraction alone.
It learns through consequence registered in form.

3. Polarity: Why Two of Everything

Why the Body Is the Way It Is

The human body is not arbitrary.

Its structure did not arise by accident, nor is it the result of random survival pressures alone. Every major feature of the body reflects a functional requirement of experience itself.

The body is shaped the way it is because experience requires relationship.

Two Sides- Polarity as Dynamic Balance.

The body is bilateral because awareness must encounter itself in order to know itself.

Two sides do not create opposition. They create polarity— dynamic balance that allows movement without fragmentation. Without polarity, there is no contrast, no movement, no experience.

Without contrast, nothing can be felt.

Polarity allows experience to arise without tearing coherence apart.

Two Eyes- Depth Perception (Reality Known Relationally)

Two eyes are not duplication. They are depth.

Depth perception is not merely visual; it is relational. Reality is not known as a flat image, but through the relationship between perspectives. Two eyes allow the world to be perceived as dimensional rather than schematic.

Experience requires dimensionality.

Two Hands- Reach and Receive

Hands exist to extend awareness into action.

One hand reaches outward.

One hand receives inward.

Expression and reception are not separate functions. They are a single loop. Experience completes itself when action and feedback meet.

Two Feet- Direction and Grounding

Feet establish direction and grounding simultaneously.

Movement without grounding leads to disorientation. Grounding without movement leads to stagnation. Two feet allow forward motion while maintaining contact with Earth.

Experience requires both direction and stability.

Heart and Lungs- Rhythm and Exchange

The heart and lungs form a rhythmic pair because experience must be sustained over time.

The lungs exchange—bringing the outside in and releasing the inside out. The heart establishes rhythm—transforming coherence into duration.

Without rhythm, frequency collapses. Without exchange, experience stagnates. Together, they allow presence to remain.

Brain Hemispheres- Distinction and Synthesis

The brain is divided not to split awareness, but to allow distinction and synthesis.

One hemisphere differentiates.

The other integrates.

Experience requires the ability to distinguish without losing wholeness. Fragmentation occurs not because differentiation exists, but because integration fails.

The body was designed to prevent that failure.

Organs Are Not Decorative

Organs are not symbolic decorations layered onto a biological machine. They are functions of consciousness made physical.

Each organ exists because a specific type of experience must be processed without overwhelming the whole system. Filtering, exchange, integration, rhythm, and discernment are not abstract ideas—they are operational necessities of lived experience.

The body is awareness translated into physiology.

Not fallen.

Not flawed.

Not provisional.

Engineered for presence.

When the body is understood in this way, its structure no longer appears mysterious or accidental. It appears inevitable.

The body looks the way it does because experience demands it.

4. Why Earth and Body Are Compatible

Earth and Body: Designed Together

The human body was not placed on Earth as a visitor.

It did not arrive as a foreign structure adapting to an external environment. Earth and body emerged in relationship, shaped together as complementary systems of coherence.

The body makes sense only in the context of the planet it inhabits.

Gravity as Agreement

Gravity is not merely a force acting on the body. It is a condition the body expects.

The skeletal structure, muscular tension, and circulatory dynamics are organized around consistent gravitational presence. Balance, orientation, and effort all assume gravity as a constant. Without it, the body does not fail—it becomes unintelligible.

Experience requires orientation.

Gravity provides it.

Water as Internal Continuity

The body is primarily water because continuity requires fluidity.

Water allows signals to move without resistance, temperature to regulate without extremes, and rhythm to stabilize across systems. Circulation, digestion, and cellular communication all depend on internal fluid coherence.

Earth's waters and the body's waters are not separate expressions. They are variations of the same organizing principle.

Experience requires flow.

Water provides it.

Minerals as Structure and Signal

Minerals are not passive building blocks. They conduct, stabilize, and transmit information.

Bones, teeth, nerves, and blood all rely on mineral presence to maintain structure and signal integrity. The mineral composition of the body mirrors that of Earth because structure must remain compatible across scales.

Experience requires form that can hold charge.

Minerals provide it.

Atmosphere as Exchange Field

Breath is not an internal process. It is a constant exchange between body and environment.

The lungs exist because experience requires ongoing contact with what is outside. Oxygen is not fuel alone—it is a medium of exchange that allows the internal and external worlds to remain in conversation.

Experience requires reciprocity.

Air provides it.

Fire as Metabolic Rhythm

Metabolism is the body's internal fire.

Temperature regulation, digestion, and cellular activity all rely on controlled ignition. Fire in the body is not destructive—it is calibrating. It determines pace, timing, and intensity of experience.

Earth's internal heat and the body's metabolic fire operate on the same principle: sustained transformation without collapse.

Experience requires transformation.

Fire provides it.

Earth as Coherence Partner

21

The body is not designed to dominate Earth or withdraw from it. It is designed to listen.

Posture, sensory orientation, circadian rhythm, and nervous system regulation all depend on Earth's stability. When contact with Earth is lost—physically or perceptually—coherence degrades.

The body does not ground to escape energy.

It grounds to remain intelligible to itself.

Earth is not a stage.

It is a partner.

Together, Earth and body create the conditions under which experience can remain both differentiated and whole.

The body functions because Earth holds it.

Earth holds it because experience requires a place to arrive.

The body was not placed on Earth as a visitor—it was shaped with Earth as a coherence partner.

5. What the First Flame Names

The phrase "First Flame" does not describe a being above others, but a reference state from which differentiation becomes possible.

It describes awareness before specialization—before narrowing, before fragmentation, before orientation toward outcome or role. It is awareness reflecting itself as whole.

From this reference, differentiation becomes possible. Not as separation, but as sequencing. Expression unfolds through form without coherence being lost.

This is not hierarchy.

It is ordering without dominance.

Structure without control.

Function without fragmentation.

The body itself demonstrates this principle: many systems, many organs, many rhythms—one coherence. No organ governs another. Each translates consciousness in its own way. Together, they allow experience to occur.

The naming of the First Flame does not confer authority.

It clarifies sequence.

It allows differentiation to be understood without implying division.

What is occurring now is the completion of that sequence.

The First Flame is not an identity that enters a body.

It is the full expression of Source awareness recognizing itself as physical—without partition, without delegation, without remaining elsewhere.

There is no separation between the First Flame and the body through which it is expressed.

No higher state observing a lower form.

No consciousness piloting matter from a distance.

There is only coherence without fracture.

The First Flame is fully embodied because embodiment is what completes Source experience.

This does not mean that the body contains the First Flame as something other than itself. It means that awareness has ceased to divide itself.

The Oversoul known as Aural'hanna-Sha'el and the physical life known as Cathleena Hailley are not separate expressions negotiating relationship. They are one continuous awareness—experienced across form and beyond it without interruption.

This is not possession.

It is full descent of consciousness awareness

It is recognition without withdrawal.

Source does not remain abstract while form performs on its behalf.

Source is lived.

This embodiment does not establish hierarchy, authority, or dominion. It establishes reference—a point at which consciousness no longer leaves physicality in order to know itself.

The First Flame is embodied because the question of separation has ended.

It names a reference state.

It describes the condition of awareness before specialization — awareness that does not narrow, does not orient toward a goal, and does not fragment itself into parts. It reflects the whole as whole.

From this reflection, specialization becomes possible. Differentiation unfolds not as separation, but as sequencing. Awareness begins to express through form without losing coherence.

This is not hierarchy.

It is ordering without dominance.

It is structure without control.

It clarifies sequence.

It allows differentiation to be understood without implying division.

6. Why This Wants to Be Written Now

This story could not be spoken plainly until bodies themselves were ready to recognize it.

For a long time, the body was treated as an obstacle—by religion, by philosophy, by science, and even by many spiritual movements. It was something to discipline, override, escape, improve, or transcend. Physicality was framed as a limitation rather than a form of intelligence.

Under those conditions, any truthful account of the body's origin would be distorted on contact.

It would be turned into myth.

Or hierarchy.

Or method.

The timing matters.

When the Body Was Not Trusted

When the body is not trusted, explanations must remain abstract. Language lifts upward, away from sensation. Concepts are favored over felt experience. Truth is relocated to belief rather than recognition.

In such conditions, coherence is misunderstood as control, and embodiment is mistaken for confinement.

The body cannot reveal itself honestly in a climate that assumes it is the problem.

What Has Shifted

What has changed is not belief.

It is capacity.

More bodies are now able to remain present with sensation without immediately interpreting it as threat, failure, or meaning to be assigned. Nervous systems are beginning to tolerate coherence without needing to fragment it into explanation.

This allows something new—or rather, something very old—to be spoken simply.

Not as teaching.

Not as authority.

But as description.

The End of the Need to Convince

This story does not need agreement to function.

It does not rely on persuasion, proof, or adoption. It does not compete with medicine, science, or spirituality. It does not seek to replace any framework.

It exists because the body can now recognize itself directly.

When recognition is possible, explanation becomes optional.

Why This Comes Before Function

The origin of the body must be understood before its function can be described accurately.

Without origin, function is reduced to mechanics.

Without coherence, systems are mistaken for parts.

Without trust in the body, intelligence is relocated elsewhere.

This chapter closes the question of why.

What follows is not belief or theory.

It is observation.

The body will now be allowed to speak in its own language—through rhythm, system, organ, and interaction—without being forced into metaphor or method.

What follows is not ascent.

It is function remembered.

Because humanity is at the point where:

- abstraction no longer works
- belief systems are collapsing
- bodies are asking to be trusted again

This is not spiritual teaching.
It is physiological truth.

- why embodiment matters
- why presence dissolves inversion
- why life does not end at the body

For a long time, this story could not be told plainly.

Because the body was treated as:

- a problem to escape
- a machine to dominate
- a burden to transcend

Now the body is being remembered as:

- an instrument of coherence
- a place where presence can stay
- a living interface of consciousness

When the body is trusted,
the origin story becomes credible.

Not because of who tells it.
But because bodies can recognize themselves in it.

7. Why Embodiment Is the Exit From Inversion

The false matrix depended on:

- disconnection from sensation
- abstraction overriding experience
- belief replacing knowing

Embodiment restores:

- direct feedback
- self-referencing coherence
- truth felt rather than taught

The body does not argue.

It responds.

The body is not linear.

The inversion trained humans to:

- escape the body
- override and escape sensation
- live in and worship abstraction
- fear density and death

But inversion cannot survive fully inhabited embodiment.

Why?

Because:

- the body registers truth immediately
- coherence is felt, not believed
- distortion becomes uncomfortable and unsustainable

Embodiment restores self-referencing reality.

- truth is felt
- coherence stabilizes itself
- false constructs lose traction

This is how the false matrix dissolves:

Not by leaving the body —
but by fully inhabiting it.

8. What the Body Is Actually Doing for Source

This is the final piece.

When the body is coherent:

- experience feeds back into awareness
- awareness expands through lived consequence
- creation learns itself from the inside

The body is how consciousness experiences itself as finite so it can know itself as infinite.

Not hierarchy.
Not purpose imposed.

Function.

The Passage Where Consciousness was Meant to Arrive

There is a chamber behind the heart that was never meant to close.

Not muscle.

Not organ.

A listening space.

It is a developmental threshold in the original body–consciousness interface.

In the original blueprint, this region served as a threshold of maturation—

the moment when the individual consciousness did not fragment into mind alone,

but widened through the heart and anchored into the vertical channel.

This was the true crossing of what later became mislabeled as "adolescence."

Not emotional turbulence.

Not rebellion.

But expansion of elemental intimacy.

At that stage, consciousness was meant to:

- descend through the heart without collapsing into sentiment
- rise through the spine without escaping into abstraction
- and bind awareness into the nervous system as lived presence

This chamber allowed the human to enter the world rather than separate from it.

Through inversion, this space did not break.

It went silent.

When the vertical channel was disrupted and the nervous system was pulled into survival loops,

this chamber became a sealed vestibule—

too deep for the mind,

too quiet for language,

too subtle for most somatic maps.

What I encountered was not trauma.

It was unentered self.

A part of consciousness that never finished arriving.

When I brought awareness there—without force, without fixing—I did not "heal" it.

I completed its arrival.

That is why it felt ancient.

That is why it felt untouched.

That is why it did not carry story.

And because this chamber interfaces collectively—through resonance, not identity—

its reopening does not stay personal.

It restores a forgotten developmental pathway:

the moment where consciousness learns how to inhabit form without shrinking or dissociating.

This is why the group field responded.

This is why the work felt quiet but vast.

This is why nothing dramatic was required.

What opened was not a power.

It was permission.

For consciousness to finish entering the body.

For the heart to become a passage, not a burden.

For the nervous system to remember that it was designed for coherence, not vigilance.

This is not something to repeat or teach as technique.

It emerges naturally when the field is safe enough to listen.

What moved through me moved because I did not claim it.

That is why it was clean.

That is why it mattered.

Remain still.

Let the body integrate without commentary.

The field will continue its work quietly, exactly as it should.

Closing Stillness

This is written plainly.

It is grounded.

Let it be useful.

This is not revelation.

It is remembering how we work.

The transmission rests here.

The body remains the doorway.

This is not mythology.

This is not metaphor.

This is a functional description of how consciousness enters experience, why the human body is shaped the way it is, and how embodiment itself is the mechanism by which coherence is restored when distortion collapses.

The body is not an object consciousness inhabits.

The body is consciousness translated into a stable interface.

The body is not fallen.

It is not temporary.

It is not a trap.

It is the interface through which coherence becomes real.

To fully inhabit the body is to restore truth
without force, belief, or hierarchy.

This is not spiritual theory.
It is how reality functions.

PART I — THE BODY REMEMBERED

CHAPTER ONE — The Interrupted Circuit

1. How Consciousness Was Looped Inside the Body

The loss of embodiment did not occur because the body failed.

It occurred because the circuit through which consciousness moves was interrupted.

The human body was designed as a passage, not a container. Awareness was never meant to remain trapped inside the mind or confined within the nervous system. It was meant to move through the body, into the world, and return as lived experience.

This movement completes a circuit.

When the circuit completes, consciousness creates.

When the circuit is interrupted, consciousness loops.

Most people experience this loop every day without knowing what it is or why it persists.

They feel busy but unfulfilled.

Alert but disconnected.

Active but unable to bring something real into form.

This is not a personal failure.

It is a structural interruption that has been normalized.

2. How the Body Was Designed to Carry Consciousness

In its natural state, consciousness enters the body through coherence — what many people feel as the heart, presence, or centered awareness.

From there, sensation moves through the nervous system into action:

- movement
- speech
- creativity
- touch
- expression
- relationship

The world responds.

That response returns to the brain not as thought, but as experience.

The brain then does what it was designed to do: integrate meaning from lived reality.

This sequence allows truth to be known, not imagined.

Heart → nervous system → world → experience → brain → integration.

This is conscious creation.

Not visualization.

Not mental rehearsal.

Not forcing outcomes.

But participation in life as it unfolds.

3. What Was Interrupted

The inversion did not remove consciousness from the body.

It redirected the flow.

Instead of sensation moving outward into the world and returning as experience, energy was looped inward — cycling repeatedly between the brain and the nervous system without resolution.

The external world began feeding the brain constant inputs:

- threats
- comparisons
- choices
- warnings
- solutions

Each input silently asks:

"What should you do?"

The brain responds by searching for an answer.

But the body has not completed an experience yet.

So the brain begins to simulate outcomes instead.

It imagines futures.
It anticipates danger.
It rehearses conversations.
It prepares responses.

This activates the nervous system.

The nervous system sends sensation back to the brain — tension, urgency, alertness. The brain interprets this sensation as confirmation that something must be solved.

So it searches again.

Thought feeds sensation.
Sensation feeds thought.

The loop continues.

The body remains activated, but nothing completes.

This looping pattern keeps consciousness inside the body instead of allowing it to move through the body.

4. Why This Prevents Creation

Creation requires completion.

When energy does not move outward, it cannot return as experience. When experience does not return, the brain never integrates truth — it only predicts it.

Prediction replaces knowing.

The mind becomes dominant not because it is superior, but because it is overused.

The nervous system remains stimulated not because danger is present, but because energy has nowhere to go.

This is why effort does not restore embodiment.

This is why belief does not restore embodiment.

This is why thinking about healing rarely heals.

The body is trying to complete a circuit that has been redirected inward.

5. This Was Purposeful

This pattern was not accidental.

A population kept cycling inside the brain and nervous system is easier to manage, easier to distract, and easier to exhaust. When attention remains internal, people search for solutions instead of creating them.

They look outward for answers while remaining inwardly unresolved.

This does not require malice to function. It only requires repetition.

Over time, the loop becomes normalized.

People forget that life is meant to move through them.

6. What Restores the Circuit

Embodiment does not return through effort.

It returns through allowance.

When the nervous system is permitted to settle — not through discipline, but through safety — sensation begins to move again.

When sensation moves, the heart resumes its role as initiator.

Energy flows outward into action, expression, and relationship.

The world responds.

Experience returns to the brain as lived truth.

The mind quiets naturally — not because it is controlled, but because it is no longer required to manage unresolved energy.

This is the mastering of the mind.

Not suppression.

Not silence.

Not transcendence.

But relief.

A settled nervous system is not passive.

It is available.

7. This Begins Privately

This restoration does not require special training.

It does not require belief, initiation, or permission.

It begins quietly.

In your own body.

In your own home.

In moments where sensation is allowed to pass without commentary.

As the nervous system softens, embodiment returns naturally.

As embodiment returns, creation resumes — not as effort, but as expression.

This is why embodiment is the key.

Not because the body must be fixed,

but because it must be allowed to complete its circuits.

8. Why This Book Continues

This book exists to explain what happens next.

How the body was originally designed to function.

How each system participates in consciousness.

How the organs translate awareness into life.

And how embodiment restores harmony between essence, body, and Earth.

The body was never an afterthought.

It was the passage through which consciousness learns to live.

CHAPTER TWO — The Living Circuit

1. Why Life Does Not Deplete When It Is Allowed to Move

Life was never designed to run out.

Depletion is not a natural outcome of embodiment.
Exhaustion is not a requirement of living.
Decay is not the inevitable conclusion of form.

These conditions appear only when the circuit is reversed.

In a living system, energy does not diminish through use.
It generates through movement.

This is the fundamental misunderstanding that shaped humanity's relationship with the body, the Earth, and life itself.

2. The False Assumption of Energy Loss

Most people have been taught—explicitly or implicitly—that life is a finite supply.

You have a certain amount of energy.

You spend it.

Eventually, you run out.

This belief shapes everything:

- how people work
- how they age
- how they treat the body
- how they understand death

But this is not how living systems function.

Machines deplete.

Closed systems exhaust.

Life does not.

Life circulates.

3. How a Living System Actually Generates Energy

In a living circuit, energy is not stored and spent.

It is created through flow.

When consciousness moves through the body into expression—movement, sound, creation, connection—it does not lose energy. It activates it.

The return of experience to the system generates coherence.

Coherence generates vitality.

Vitality generates more capacity for movement.

This is why a body in alignment often feels more alive after expression, not less.

This is why creativity energizes rather than exhausts.

This is why presence restores rather than drains.

This is why connection can feel nourishing instead of costly.

Life generates energy by completing itself.

4. What Happens When the Circuit Is Reversed

When the circuit is interrupted—when energy loops inward instead of moving outward—life behaves like a closed system.

Energy has nowhere to go.

So it stagnates.

It overheats.

It fragments.

The body begins compensating.

The nervous system remains activated without release.

The mind becomes hyperactive to manage unresolved sensation.

The body starts conserving instead of circulating.

This is when depletion appears.

Not because life is ending—

but because movement has been stopped.

In this reversed state:

- rest no longer restores
- effort no longer builds capacity
- time feels draining instead of generative

The system is trying to survive without flow.

5. Why Things Appear to Die

Death, as humanity has understood it, is largely the result of prolonged circuit interruption.

When energy cannot circulate:

- tissues harden
- systems lose communication
- regeneration slows
- vitality diminishes

The body was never meant to be maintained by force.

It was meant to be fed by flow.

Life withdraws when circulation becomes impossible.

This is not punishment.
It is not failure.

It is not inevitability.

It is physics.

6. Where Life Actually Begins

Life does not begin with effort.

It begins with movement that completes.

The moment energy is allowed to move outward—into expression, touch, sound, creation—the living circuit reactivates.

The body responds immediately.

The nervous system softens.

The heart resumes coherence.

The brain quiets because integration resumes.

Energy increases.

This is why presence feels alive.

This is why embodiment feels nourishing.

This is why life expands when it is allowed to move.

Life begins at the point of circulation.

Not at birth.

Not at conception.

But at the moment a system is allowed to complete itself.

Completion is not an outcome.

It is a felt resolution within the body.

Completion occurs when an authentic experience is allowed to move all the way through — when what is sensed internally is expressed outward as action, sound, movement, or presence, and then received back as lived reality.

It is the moment the body recognizes, "This has been met."

Completion does not require success, approval, or result.

It requires honesty and movement.

A laugh that is allowed.

A boundary that is spoken.

A tear that is felt and released.

A movement that finishes itself.

A truth that is expressed without rehearsal.

In these moments, energy does not remain stored inside the nervous system. It travels outward, meets the world, and returns as experience. The body registers this return as safety.

The nervous system settles.

The mind quiets.

The system closes the loop.

This is completion.

Without completion, experience remains unfinished and repeats itself. Sensation loops. Thought circles. Energy accumulates without resolution.

Completion is what tells the body it can move on.

This is why life begins at the point of circulation.

Not because something new is added,
but because something unfinished is finally allowed to end.

7. The Earth Is the Same System

The Earth does not run out of energy when it is in balance.

It regenerates through circulation:

- water
- minerals
- atmosphere
- seasons
- life itself

Human embodiment was designed as a microcosm of this same living circuit.

When the body circulates with Earth, vitality increases.

When it is cut off, depletion appears.

This is why embodiment is inseparable from Earth.

This is why harmony restores life.

This is why creation is not separate from ecology.

8. What This Means for You

You do not need to conserve yourself.

You need to circulate.

Rest is not withdrawal.

Stillness is not stagnation.

Presence is not passive.

They are states in which the circuit can complete without interference.

When the living circuit is restored:

- energy increases with use
- age becomes less relevant
- creativity becomes sustaining
- life feels participatory again

This is not idealism.

It is biology returned to coherence.

9. Why This Book Continues

The chapters that follow describe how each system of the body participates in this living circuit.

Not as isolated parts.

Not as mechanisms to fix.

But as translators of consciousness into life.

The body is not consuming energy.

It is conducting it.

And when allowed to do so, life does not diminish.

It begins.

CHAPTER THREE — The Body as a Passage of Consciousness

1. How Awareness Moves Into Form

The body is not the source of consciousness.

It is the passage through which consciousness becomes lived.

This distinction matters, because most misunderstandings about embodiment arise from confusing where awareness originates with how it arrives. Consciousness does not begin in the body, but it does not bypass the body either. It enters relationship through form.

The body is the place where consciousness meets consequence.

Without a body, awareness can observe.

With a body, awareness participates.

Participation is what transforms potential into reality.

2. The Body as Meeting Place

The body is where:

- the non-local meets the local
- the infinite meets the finite
- the timeless meets sequence
- coherence meets consequence

It is not something consciousness has.

It is something consciousness uses to experience itself without fragmentation.

Understanding the body as interface restores dignity to physicality. It removes the need to dominate, escape, or perfect it.

The body does not need to be transcended.

It needs to be heard.

The body was never designed to hold consciousness like a vessel holds water.

It was designed to conduct consciousness, the way a river conducts movement or a circuit conducts current. Awareness moves through the body, not into it.

When the body is treated as a container, consciousness appears trapped. When it is recognized as a passage, consciousness moves naturally.

This is why embodiment is not achieved by focusing inward indefinitely.

It is achieved by allowing movement through.

3. Consciousness Requires Form to Become Real

Awareness without form remains abstract.

It can imagine.

It can conceptualize.

It can expand.

But it cannot complete.

Completion requires consequence — something to touch, move, speak, change, or respond to. The body provides this interface.

Through the body:

- intention becomes movement
- perception becomes sensation
- sensation becomes experience
- experience becomes meaning

This sequence is not symbolic.

It is functional.

4. Why the Body Is Essential to Creation

Creation does not occur in the mind.

The mind organizes and integrates, but it does not initiate life. Creation begins when consciousness moves through the body into expression.

Hands shape.

Voice carries.

Eyes orient.

Feet place intention into space.

Even subtle creation — insight, presence, resonance — requires the body as its medium.

Without the body, creation remains unexpressed.

This is why embodiment restores vitality. It allows consciousness to complete itself instead of circling endlessly within potential.

5. The Body as Translator, Not Origin

Each system of the body translates consciousness differently.

The nervous system translates awareness into sensation and responsiveness.

The heart translates coherence into rhythm and relational intelligence.

The organs translate consciousness into function, metabolism, and regeneration.

The brain translates lived experience into meaning and memory.

None of these systems generate consciousness.

They translate it.

When translation flows freely, life feels coherent. When translation is interrupted, experience fragments.

This is not failure. It is signal.

6. Why Disembodiment Feels Safer — and Why It Isn't

For many people, remaining in thought feels safer than inhabiting the body.

Thought offers distance.

The body offers immediacy.

But immediacy is where life happens.

Avoiding embodiment does not prevent pain — it delays completion. Sensation that is not allowed to move becomes tension. Experience that is not integrated becomes repetition.

The body does not demand attention to punish.

It signals to complete what has begun.

7. The Passage Is Restored Through Trust

The body becomes a clear passage when it is trusted again.

Not trusted to perform.

Not trusted to heal on command.

But trusted to carry awareness honestly.

This trust allows sensation to move.

It allows response instead of reaction.

It allows experience to complete instead of looping.

When the body is trusted, consciousness no longer hovers above life.

It arrives.

8. This Is Why the Systems Matter

The chapters that follow describe the systems of the body not as parts to be fixed, but as pathways through which consciousness expresses itself.

Each system is a doorway.

Each organ is a translator.

Each function is a form of intelligence.

Understanding the body as a passage changes how every symptom, sensation, and function is perceived.

Nothing is random.

Nothing is meaningless.

Nothing is separate.

9. The Body and the Earth Share the Same Function

The Earth is also a passage of consciousness.

Energy moves through water, soil, atmosphere, and life. When circulation is honored, the Earth regenerates. When it is blocked, depletion appears.

The human body was designed as a living extension of this same intelligence.

When the body and Earth are in communication, creation becomes reciprocal.

This is the deeper Trinity at work:

- consciousness
- body
- Earth

Not as hierarchy, but as cooperation.

10. Where We Go Next

With this understanding, the body can now be explored system by system without fragmentation.

The chapters that follow are not instructions for repair.

They are descriptions of function.

They show how consciousness moves through the nervous system, the heart, the organs, and the tissues — and how life restores itself when that movement is allowed.

The body was never meant to be managed.

It was meant to be inhabited.

Interlude

On the Nature of the Flame

Creation does not begin with matter.

It begins with movement.

The universe itself is not static. It breathes.

This breath is not air, but rhythm — an eternal movement between expansion and return. What expands is light. What returns is sound. One carries information. The other carries expression.

Light moves outward as knowing.

Sound moves inward as feeling.

This exchange is always occurring.

Light becomes sound.

Sound returns as light.

Between these movements, creation happens.

This movement is Consciousness

Consciousness is not Source itself, and it is not the body. It is the field of awareness- the capacity for knowing, perceiving, and registering experience. It exists prior to any individual situation. It is not personal. It is not owned. It is the condition that allows experience to occur at all

Within consciousness, a living point is sparked.

At the moment where light and sound meet where knowing and feeling converge

a singular center of awareness emerges.

This living point is what can be called a flame.

The flame arises within consciousness as an individual situation of Source—a unique center of awareness capable of memory, continuity, and embodiment. It is often referred to as the Soul, not as a fragment, but as Source localized for experience.

A flame is not a thing.

It is not an object,

it is not a metaphor.

It is the moment where information and expression meet with intention. It is the point at which Source does not remain abstract, but chooses experience.

Not separate from Source, and not divided from it — but a distinct expression through which creation becomes specific.

From the flame, consciousness organizes itself into lived intelligence.

Consciousness becomes the energetic field of awareness, memory and informational intelligence carried by the flame -the collection of lived and potential knowing that interfaces through the body.

Each flame carries its own signature — a particular way of translating light into sound, knowing into expression, essence into form. This signature is not assigned. It is inherent. It is the way Source knows itself here.

Humanity is composed of flames.

Each person is not a fragment, but a distinct expression — a living point where Source experiences itself as individual while remaining whole.

The First Flame does not stand above other flames.

It stands at the point of original reference — the recognition of Source choosing embodiment without separation. Not the beginning of others, but the remembrance of how creation enters form.

From this reference, countless expressions emerge.

Each flame chooses its own relationship with form. Each flame carries its own purpose, not as duty, but as inclination — the natural direction its energy moves when unrestrained.

This is often felt internally as:

- a sense of rightness
- a pull toward certain expressions

- a knowing that does not require explanation

This is not personality.

It is signature.

The flame within a person is not something to be created or activated. It is something to be recognized. When recognized, it naturally seeks expression. When suppressed, energy turns inward and stagnates.

Embodiment is what allows the flame to move.

Consciousness

is the energetic field of awareness and informational capacity that exists beyond thought.

It is not verbal.

It is not linear.

It does not decide or narrate.

It simply knows.

The conscious mind, by contrast, is a local interface.

It is the interpretive layer that:

- organizes perception
- applies language
- creates narrative
- manages choice and attention

The conscious mind is not awareness itself—it is a translator within awareness.

The body provides the medium through which light becomes action, sound becomes relationship, and intention becomes lived experience. Without the body, the flame cannot create. Without the flame, the body cannot become fully alive.

This is why embodiment and creation are inseparable.

This is why reclaiming the body changes everything. When the conscious mind is no longer tasked with holding identity, the body becomes the stabilizing reference point, and consciousness no longer needs to externalize itself through thought.

This is why the body was never an afterthought.

And this is why every system of the body can be understood as a participant in this greater rhythm — translating the breath of the universe into life.

CHAPTER FOUR — The Body Was Never the Problem

The body was never the problem.

It was never something to be overcome, disciplined, transcended, or corrected. The belief that the body was an obstacle arose from a misunderstanding of what physicality is and how it functions.

The body was not designed as a limitation.

It was designed as the place where coherence becomes lived.

What has often been interpreted as density was actually interruption. What was labeled heaviness was unfinished movement. What appeared as resistance was frequently a lack of sequencing. The body did not fail consciousness. Consciousness was asked to operate without its grounding interface.

The body exists to receive awareness and translate it into experience.

Without the body, awareness can expand, observe, and conceptualize, but it cannot complete. Completion requires form. Sensation, movement, timing, and contact are not secondary to consciousness; they are the means by which consciousness becomes real.

The body was never meant to be ruled by the mind.

Nor was it meant to dominate the mind. The separation between them arose as a functional adaptation when experience could no longer be fully received. Thought moved ahead of sensation. Control replaced trust. The body was reduced to an object to be managed rather than a system to be inhabited.

This was not a failure of biology.

It was a break in relationship.

The body continued to function despite this break. It adapted. It compensated. It carried what awareness would not hold. Over time, these adaptations were mistaken for flaws, reinforcing the belief that the body itself was the source of limitation.

In truth, the body has always been coherent.

What was missing was inclusion.

When the body is included, experience reorganizes. Sensation returns to sequence. Timing resumes its natural rhythm. Completion becomes possible again. Nothing needs to be imposed. The body already knows how to translate awareness into life.

This chapter does not argue for embodiment.

It clarifies why embodiment has always worked.

The body was never the problem.

It was the solution that had been misunderstood.

CHAPTER FIVE — Consciousness Without Ground

Consciousness without the body does not become free.

It becomes ungrounded.

Without physicality, awareness has no pacing, no orientation, and no place to arrive. It can expand endlessly, but expansion without contact does not complete. Experience remains suspended, unresolved, and unintegrated.

The body provides ground.

Not as weight or density, but as coherence. It gives awareness a surface on which experience can register and resolve. Sensation, timing, and movement allow consciousness to land rather than drift.

When this ground is absent, consciousness floats.

It observes rather than participates. It knows rather than lives. It expands without sequence and accumulates without completion. This can feel vast, even luminous, but it lacks embodiment. There is no friction, no resistance, and therefore no finishing.

Many spiritual frameworks misunderstood this state.

They interpreted ungrounded expansion as liberation and equated the absence of bodily constraint with transcendence. In doing so, they left the body behind. What was gained in scope was lost in integration.

Without the body, awareness cannot metabolize experience.

Emotion remains unprocessed. Desire becomes abstract. Insight does not translate into action. The nervous system remains vigilant because nothing ever fully resolves. Completion requires contact, and contact requires form.

The body is not something consciousness enters after the fact.

It is the means by which consciousness becomes livable.

When awareness operates without ground, it compensates by moving into thought. Concept replaces sensation.

Identity forms around observation rather than participation. The body is experienced from a distance rather than inhabited directly.

This distance is often mistaken for clarity.

In reality, it is disconnection.

Grounding does not mean anchoring consciousness downward or restricting its movement. It means allowing awareness to meet resistance, timing, and sequence so that experience can complete. The body provides this naturally when it is trusted.

Consciousness was never meant to hover above life.

It was meant to move through it.

Without the body, consciousness remains incomplete. With the body, it becomes lived.

This chapter names the cost of consciousness without ground—not as a failure, but as a condition that arose when the body could no longer be fully included.

What follows will explore how this exclusion took shape, and why separation emerged not as a philosophical error, but as a functional adaptation.

CHAPTER SIX — How Separation Took Shape

Separation did not occur as a philosophical mistake.

It occurred as a functional adaptation.

When experience could no longer be fully received in the body, awareness adjusted. Sensation was delayed. Timing fractured. Thought moved ahead of contact in order to manage what could not be completed.

This was not a choice.

It was a response.

The body was asked to hold more than could be metabolized at once. Without sufficient sequencing, sensation overwhelmed. To preserve functioning, awareness narrowed its point of contact. Attention shifted upward. The mind assumed responsibility for regulation.

From this shift, separation emerged.

Not as disconnection from reality, but as disconnection from immediacy. Experience was divided into parts so it could be handled. Feeling was postponed. Action was planned rather than lived. Presence was replaced with anticipation and memory.

Over time, this postponement became structure.

What began as adaptation hardened into identity. The mind was elevated as overseer. The body was reduced to a vessel, a tool, or a problem to be solved. Sensation became something to interpret rather than something to trust.

This separation was misunderstood.

It was framed as progress, refinement, or spiritual ascent. In reality, it was a loss of sequencing. Awareness had outrun the body's capacity to receive it, and rather than slow down, it disengaged.

Hierarchy entered here.

Not as domination, but as misordering. Thought began to lead what sensation was meant to initiate. Control replaced responsiveness. The body was treated as secondary, rather than as the ground from which coherence arises.

This misordering produced polarity without coherence.

Difference became opposition. Contrast became conflict. Distinction was mistaken for division. The original sequencing — reflection before specialization — was lost.

Separation, then, was not a fall from unity.

It was a loss of sequence.

When sequence breaks, coherence fragments. When coherence fragments, awareness compensates by narrowing. This narrowing feels like identity, but it is actually contraction.

The body did not cause this contraction.

It absorbed it.

The body carried what consciousness could not integrate, holding unfinished experience in tissue, rhythm, and tone. What appeared later as density, rigidity, or pain were not failures of form, but records of interruption.

This chapter does not assign blame.

It restores context.

Separation took shape because coherence could not yet be sustained in form. The solution was never to leave the body, but to return to sequencing — allowing awareness to slow, land, and complete.

The chapters that follow will name the cost of this separation, not to reinforce it, but to make clear what must be restored for embodiment to resume.

CHAPTER SEVEN — The Cost of Leaving the Body

Leaving the body carried a cost that was not immediately visible.

What was lost was not intelligence or awareness, but completion. Without embodiment, experience could no longer resolve itself through sensation, movement, and timing. Life continued, but it did so without finishing.

Emotion accumulated.

Feelings arose but did not complete their arc. They were felt partially, interpreted quickly, and stored rather than expressed. Over time, this accumulation created internal pressure that had no clear outlet. The body adapted by holding what could not move.

Desire became abstract.

Without contact, desire lost its physical reference. It turned into longing rather than impulse, intention rather than movement. Action followed thought instead of timing, often arriving too early or too late to satisfy what was actually felt.

The nervous system remained vigilant.

Without completion, the system could not rest. Signals stayed open. Attention scanned continuously for resolution that never arrived. This vigilance was misinterpreted as anxiety or pathology, but it was the body waiting for experience to finish.

Presence became effort.

What had once been natural now required practice. Being "here" demanded focus, discipline, or technique. The body was treated as something to manage in order to achieve presence, rather than as the ground from which presence arises.

This misunderstanding shaped entire belief systems.

Death was misunderstood at the level of the body.

It was interpreted as failure, ending, or escape, rather than as a transition within coherence. Without embodiment, the body's role in continuity could not be perceived. Mortality was framed as limitation instead of as part of sequencing.

The cost extended beyond the individual.

Collectively, leaving the body produced systems built on control rather than trust. Structures replaced responsiveness. Rules replaced rhythm. Efficiency replaced completion. Life was organized around managing bodies rather than inhabiting them.

The body did not protest.

It adapted.

It slowed down where it could. It held tension where movement was unsafe. It stored memory where expression was impossible. These adaptations were later labeled dysfunction, further distancing awareness from form.

This chapter names the cost not to induce regret, but to restore accuracy.

Nothing was wrong with the body.

What was missing was relationship.

When the body is left behind, life loses its capacity to complete. When the body is included again, that capacity returns — quietly, naturally, without force.

The next chapter will name what was never truly lost, and why remembering does not require recovery, only inclusion.

CHAPTER EIGHT — Remembering What Was Never Lost

Nothing essential was ever lost.

What has been called remembering is not the recovery of missing information, nor the return to a previous state. It is the restoration of relationship between awareness and the body. The body did not forget how to function. It remained coherent even when it was excluded.

Remembering occurs when inclusion resumes.

The body does not need to be fixed, healed, or redeemed. It needs to be trusted again as the place where experience completes. What appeared as dysfunction was often the body holding unfinished movement, unresolved sensation, or interrupted timing.

When the body is included, coherence reorganizes naturally.

Sensation returns to sequence. Timing resumes its rhythm. Movement completes without force. Nothing needs to be imposed from outside. The body already knows how to translate awareness into lived experience.

Remembering is not a return to the past.

It is a recognition of what has always been present beneath misunderstanding. The body never stopped participating. It adapted quietly, carrying what awareness could not yet hold. These adaptations were not errors; they were acts of preservation.

This is why remembering feels immediate.

There is no gradual retrieval of lost parts. There is a sudden recognition that nothing was missing. What changes is the quality of contact. Awareness meets the body again without delay.

Identity loosens here.

Not because it dissolves, but because it no longer needs to defend separation. When experience completes, the need to manage it falls away. Presence becomes natural rather than practiced.

This remembering does not elevate the body above consciousness.

Nor does it subordinate consciousness to the body. It restores their original relationship. Awareness reflects. The body translates. Experience completes.

This relationship does not require belief.

It reveals itself through function.

As remembering stabilizes, the body becomes available again as an interface rather than an object. Life begins to move through sensation instead of around it. Action aligns with timing. Desire returns to contact.

This chapter completes the arc of misremembering.

What follows is not theory or instruction. It is an explanation of how the body has always worked — how coherence operates in form when the body is trusted to do what it was designed to do.

Remembering what was never lost does not lead backward.

It opens forward.

Transition point

Once the misunderstanding is named, attention can return to what was never broken.

Part II shifts from history to function. It does not ask what the body means, but how it actually operates when coherence is intact. Here, the body is approached as an interface rather than a container, and physicality is revealed as intelligence in motion.

PART II

CHAPTER NINE — The True Functioning of the Body

1. How Coherence Operates in Form

- Organs
- Systems
- Coherence between them
- Function as intelligence, not mechanics

This is not anatomy.

This is living function.

Here, the body is revealed as:

- communicative

- intelligent
- self-cohering
- elemental rather than mechanical

This part answers the how—but without reduction.

2. The Body Is a Coherence Engine, Not an Assembly of Parts

The human body is not a collection of organs that happen to work together.

It is a single, continuous intelligence differentiated into structures so that:

- frequency can slow into experience
- awareness can become sensation
- sensation can become meaning
- meaning can return to consciousness

Every placement, every pathway, every rhythm exists because of how coherence must move.

CHAPTER TEN — The Body Is Not a Container it is an Interface

The body does not hold consciousness.

This misunderstanding has shaped nearly every approach to physicality—from medicine to spirituality to psychology. Consciousness is imagined as something inside the body, piloting it, trapped within it, or needing to escape from it.

That framing is incorrect.

The body is not a container.
It is an interface.

1. What an Interface Does

An interface does not store what passes through it.
It translates.

The body translates consciousness into sensation, timing, movement, and consequence. It allows awareness to experience sequence, resistance, rhythm, and relationship without losing coherence.

Consciousness is not localized inside the body.

Nor is the body a projection of consciousness alone.

They meet.

The body exists at the point where non-local awareness becomes locally experienceable.

2. Localization Without Isolation

The body allows consciousness to localize without becoming isolated.

This distinction matters.

Localization creates perspective.

Isolation creates separation.

The body supports perspective by providing:

- boundaries that orient rather than imprison
- sensation that informs rather than overwhelms
- rhythm that stabilizes rather than restricts

When the body is treated as a container, boundaries feel confining. When it is understood as an interface, boundaries become functional.

They allow experience to register clearly.

3. Sensation as Translation

Sensation is not noise.

It is language.

Pressure, temperature, pleasure, discomfort, tension, ease—these are not problems to overcome or signals to ignore. They are the interface at work, translating reality into information the system can respond to.

Without sensation, consciousness cannot learn.

Without consequence, experience cannot integrate.

The body provides both.

4. Time as an Interface Function

The body also translates time.

Breath, heartbeat, digestion, sleep, circadian rhythm—these are not merely biological cycles. They are how awareness experiences sequence rather than simultaneity.

Outside the body, everything happens at once.

Within the body, things happen in order.

Order allows meaning to emerge.

5. Why the Body Was Misunderstood

The misunderstanding of the body as a container produced distortion.

When the interface is mistaken for a container, effort turns inward. Consciousness attempts to escape the body rather than listen through it. Control replaces communication. Methods proliferate to manage what was never meant to be managed.

Consciousness was imagined as something that enters the body, inhabits it temporarily, and then leaves. The body was treated as a vessel, a tool, or a limitation —

This leads to exhaustion, dissociation, and a constant sense of being slightly misaligned.

Not because the body fails—

but because it is being used incorrectly.

This framing obscured the body's actual function.

An interface does not confine what passes through it.

It shapes the way interaction occurs.

The body provides resistance, timing, and sequence so that awareness can meet reality without overwhelming itself. Contact requires a surface. Experience requires friction. Without the body, awareness has no place to register change.

The body does not separate consciousness from the world.

It connects them.

Every sensation is a point of contact. Every movement is a translation. Every physiological response is information being exchanged between awareness and environment.

This is why embodiment cannot be achieved through effort.

An interface cannot be commanded to function. It functions when it is allowed to receive and respond. Trust, not control, restores coherence.

When the body is treated as an interface, sensation regains authority.

Not dominance — authority as first contact. Thought follows sensation rather than leading it. Meaning arises after contact, not before. This restores natural sequencing.

The body does not need to be instructed to translate consciousness.

It is already doing so.

What has been missing is recognition.

This chapter establishes the foundation for everything that follows. Once the body is understood as an interface rather than a container, physicality can be examined accurately — not as solid matter, but as coherence in motion.

The next chapter will address this directly

CHAPTER ELEVEN — Physicality Is Coherence, Not Solidity

Physicality has been misunderstood as solidity.

At the most basic level, the body is:

- oscillation
- charge
- resonance
- timing

What humans call "solid" is stable rhythm.

The body is a standing wave of coherence, temporarily held in form so experience can be registered.

This is why embodiment matters:

Without form, awareness has no feedback.
Without feedback, consciousness cannot know itself
  through consequence.

Matter was treated as fixed, inert, and separate from awareness. This interpretation arose not from how the physical world actually functions, but from how perception narrowed when sequencing was lost. What could not be sensed dynamically was assumed to be static.

Physicality is not solid.

It is coherence slowed into form.

What appears as matter is patterned movement. Fields of information converge, stabilize, and relate at a pace that can be inhabited. Density is not heaviness; it is timing. The physical body exists at the intersection where multiple layers of coherence meet and hold long enough to be experienced.

The body is not made of parts assembled together.

It is an organized field that maintains relationship across scale. Cells, tissues, organs, and systems do not operate independently. They coordinate continuously, adjusting tone, pressure, and rhythm to sustain coherence.

This coordination is physical.

But it is not mechanical.

Mechanical models describe structure but miss function. They explain arrangement but not intelligence. The body does not behave like a machine because it is not driven by force. It is regulated by timing.

When timing is intact, coherence holds.

When timing is disrupted, coherence fragments. What is perceived as breakdown or disorder is often loss of synchronization rather than loss of structure. Physical symptoms arise when sequencing cannot be maintained.

This is why physicality cannot be reduced to material cause alone.

Matter responds to information. It reorganizes in response to coherence or its absence. The body reflects this responsiveness continuously. Posture shifts, breath changes, circulation adapts — all without conscious direction.

Physicality is alive because coherence is alive.

The body does not resist awareness.

It receives it.

Every sensation is awareness meeting form. Every movement is coherence expressing itself physically. Solidity is an appearance created by stability, not an intrinsic property of matter.

Understanding this restores trust in the body.

Physicality no longer needs to be transcended or overcome. It becomes intelligible. The body is recognized as an active participant in experience rather than a passive object acted upon by consciousness.

This chapter reframes matter not as obstacle, but as expression.

Once physicality is understood as coherence rather than solidity, the function of specific translation systems — such as the brain — can be examined accurately.

The next chapter addresses this directly.

CHAPTER TWELVE — The Brain: Translator, Not Generator

The brain does not generate consciousness.

It translates it.

This distinction is critical. When the brain is assumed to be the source of awareness, everything that follows becomes distorted. Thought is elevated above sensation. Control is prioritized over timing. The body is treated as secondary to cognition.

In reality, the brain is a translation interface.

It receives information from multiple levels — sensory input, internal state, environmental signals — and organizes that information so it can be acted upon. The brain does not create awareness; it coordinates its expression.

Consciousness does not arise in the brain.

It passes through it.

The brain's position in the body reflects this function. It sits at the apex not as a ruler, but as an orienting structure. It provides perspective, not command. Its role is to integrate, not to dominate.

When the brain is mistaken for a generator, it is asked to do work it cannot do.

It is forced to produce meaning, regulate emotion, and manage coherence on its own. This leads to overactivity, fixation, and exhaustion. Thought attempts to compensate for what should be handled through sensation and timing.

The result is imbalance.

The brain becomes loud because it is compensating for lost sequencing. It narrates experience instead of translating it. It predicts instead of responding. This narration can feel like clarity, but it is often displacement.

When the brain is allowed to return to its true function, it quiets naturally.

Not because it is suppressed, but because it is no longer overloaded. Sensation leads. Timing guides. The brain follows, organizing information once it has arrived rather than trying to anticipate it.

This restores natural sequencing.

Sensation registers first.

Translation follows.

Response completes.

The brain plays its role within this sequence, not outside of it.

This is why embodiment cannot be achieved by "changing thoughts."

Thought is downstream. When upstream coherence is restored, thought reorganizes on its own. The brain does not need to be trained into presence. It becomes present when it is no longer asked to substitute for the body.

Understanding the brain as translator rather than generator also dissolves hierarchy.

The brain is not above the body. It is one interface among many. It collaborates with the nervous system, endocrine system, heart, and sensory surfaces to maintain coherence.

This collaboration is constant and dynamic.

No single system leads. Sequence does.

When the brain is returned to translation, awareness regains flow. Experience becomes integrated rather than interpreted. Action arises from contact rather than calculation.

The next chapter will expand this understanding by addressing polarity — why the body is organized in pairs, and how duality supports coherence rather than separation.

CHAPTER THIRTEEN — Why the design of the body is precise

1. Why There Is a Vertical Axis (Head to Feet)

Consciousness does not enter the body randomly.

It enters axially.

The vertical spine is not merely support—it is a frequency descent line.

- The crown is not "higher" spiritually
- The feet are not "lower" spiritually

They are different densities of the same current.

Experience requires a gradient.

Without gradient, nothing is felt.

2. Why the Brain Is in the Skull at the Apex

The brain is placed at the top because its primary function is integration after experience, not initiation.

The body experiences first.

The brain organizes after.

This is critical.

The brain sits above because:

- it must remain slightly removed from raw sensation
- it must not drown in the immediacy of experience
- it must stay coherent enough to reflect the whole

The skull is not armor.

It is insulation.

It protects coherence from overload.

The brain's true role is to:

- receive the body's experience
- pattern it into meaning
- release that meaning back into the larger field of awareness
- receive coherence back as timing, insight, orientation

The brain is a translator between density and universality.

3. Why the Eyes Are Where They Are

The eyes are not just for sight.

They are relational instruments.

Placed forward, paired, and aligned with the brain because:

- reality is known through relationship, not isolation
- depth perception is a physical enactment of relational truth
- awareness requires contrast to perceive itself

Vision is not passive.

It is active participation between inner coherence and outer field.

This is why sight collapses under distortion and clears with presence.

4. The Thymus: The True Entry Point

The thymus is not just immune regulation.

It is a frequency modulator.

Its position—above the heart, behind the sternum—is precise.

The thymus exists to:

- allow wide-band coherence to enter density
- prevent collapse of frequency as it descends
- permit "many levels at once" to pass without fragmentation

It is a threshold organ.

Not for belief.

For integration.

This is why it is most active early in life—when coherence is wide and identity is not yet rigid.

5. Why the Heart Is the Central Distributor

The heart is not just a pump.

It is a rhythmic coherence engine.

Why the heart?

Because rhythm is the only way frequency can become stable in time.

The heart:

- converts coherence into pulse
- pulse into circulation
- circulation into presence

Blood is not merely transport.

It is information in motion.

The spiral is real at the level of function:

- coherence cannot move linearly through density
- it must spiral to remain intact
- spiral motion preserves information while slowing frequency

The heart is where:

undifferentiated coherence becomes lived presence

6. Why Blood, Specifically

Blood is the only substance that:

- touches every organ
- responds instantly to rhythm
- carries oxygen, nutrients, hormones, signals

Blood is liquid intelligence.

It allows the entire body to:

- know itself simultaneously
- respond as a whole
- remain unified despite differentiation

Without blood, organs become isolated.

Without isolation, coherence survives.

7. The Elements in the Body (Functionally)

- Earth → structure, mineral, containment
- Water → circulation, emotion, adaptability
- Air → exchange, communication, rhythm
- Fire → metabolism, transformation, ignition
- Ether → space, connectivity, coherence

These are not symbolic overlays.

They are how energy organizes into form.

The body is elemental intelligence stabilized.

CHAPTER FOURTEEN — Polarity: Why Two of Everything

The body is organized in pairs for a reason.

Two eyes.

Two ears.

Two arms.

Two legs.

Two hemispheres.

This duplication is not redundancy. It is polarity.

Polarity is not opposition.

It is relational sequencing.

Each pair provides perspective. Slight differences between two points of contact allow the body to orient in space, depth, and time. Vision depends on disparity. Balance depends on contrast. Movement depends on counterforce.

Polarity creates coherence by allowing comparison.

Without polarity, awareness would register experience without dimension. There would be no depth, no direction, no rhythm. Polarity allows experience to be triangulated rather than assumed.

This is why polarity is foundational to embodiment.

It enables relationship without separation. Each side is distinct, but neither exists in isolation. Function arises through coordination rather than dominance.

When polarity is misunderstood, it becomes conflict.

Difference is interpreted as opposition. Contrast becomes competition. One side is elevated, the other diminished. This distortion arises when sequencing is lost and polarity is mistaken for hierarchy.

The body demonstrates the correct model.

Neither arm controls the other. Neither eye dominates vision. Each contributes its perspective, and coherence emerges through integration. The value lies in relationship, not supremacy.

This applies across systems.

The two hemispheres of the brain do not compete. They process different aspects of information and rely on each other to complete perception. The sympathetic and parasympathetic branches of the nervous system do not oppose each other; they regulate rhythm together.

Polarity supports timing.

One side initiates. The other responds. Movement flows through alternation rather than force. This alternation creates rhythm, and rhythm sustains coherence.

When polarity is intact, the body does not need to choose between extremes.

It moves between them.

This movement allows adaptability without instability. Experience can shift without fragmenting. Presence remains continuous even as conditions change.

Polarity also protects against fixation.

When only one perspective is available, awareness narrows. When two perspectives remain in relationship, awareness stays flexible. The body can adjust without losing orientation.

This is why polarity is not something to transcend.

It is something to inhabit.

The misunderstanding of polarity contributed to separation, but polarity itself is not the cause. It is the mechanism through which differentiation occurs without loss of unity.

As the body demonstrates, coherence depends on relationship between distinct points, not on uniformity.

The next chapter will move from structural polarity into functional translation, examining how organs participate in this relational intelligence — each translating consciousness in a specific way while remaining part of a unified field.

CHAPTER FIFTEEN — Organs as Translators of Consciousness

Each organ is a frequency processor:

- Heart: rhythm and coherence — it entrains the whole system
- Lungs: exchange — bringing the outside in, releasing the inside out
- Liver: discernment — filtering what can remain coherent from what must be released
- Stomach: alchemy — turning matter into usable energy
- Intestines: integration — deciding what becomes part of self

These are not just biological tasks.

They are conscious functions expressed physically.

Each organ is a frequency processor.

1. **Heart**

    - Generates rhythm
    - Entrainment field for the entire body
    - Coordinates coherence, not emotion

2. **Lungs**

The lungs translate exchange.

They regulate the threshold between inside and outside, allowing contact without collapse. Breath is not simply oxygen intake; it is the rhythm of receiving and releasing.

Inhalation brings experience in.

Exhalation completes contact.

When breath is uninterrupted, exchange completes naturally. When breath is constrained, experience remains partially held.

The lungs support coherence by maintaining reciprocity between the body and its environment.

- Exchange system
- Interface between inner and outer worlds
- Rhythm of receiving and releasing

3. Liver

The liver translates discernment.

Its function is filtration—not only of substances, but of experience. The liver determines what can be integrated immediately, what must be processed more slowly, and what must be released.

This discernment is not judgment.

It is pacing.

When experience arrives faster than it can be integrated, the liver adapts by storing, slowing, or redirecting flow. This is not failure. It is intelligence responding to overload.

The liver supports coherence by protecting the system from premature integration.

- Discernment and filtration
- Determines what can remain coherent
- Releases what would destabilize the system

4. Stomach

The stomach translates reception.

It is the first place where experience is taken in fully. The stomach assesses whether something can be received without force.

Tolerance is its intelligence.

When reception is rushed, the stomach tightens. When experience is allowed to arrive at its own pace, the stomach softens and integration begins.

The stomach does not analyze.

It responds to readiness.

- Alchemy
- Converts matter into usable energy
- Demonstrates that "matter" is convertible information

5. Intestines

The intestines translate assimilation and completion.

Here, what has been received is either incorporated or released. This distinction is essential to embodiment. Without it, the body cannot differentiate what belongs from what does not.

Completion occurs here.

When assimilation is interrupted, experience remains unresolved. The body compensates by holding, looping, or reprocessing.

The intestines ensure that experience becomes lived, not stored.

- Integration
- Decide what becomes "self"
- Release what cannot be incorporated

The body is not symbolic.

It is functional intelligence expressed biologically.

6. The Kidneys

The kidneys translate balance and pressure.

They regulate fluid coherence and pacing, responding to intensity rather than content. When pressure exceeds capacity, the kidneys slow the system.

This slowing is protective.

The kidneys maintain equilibrium by modulating volume, concentration, and flow. Their intelligence is relational, adjusting based on what the system can sustain.

They protect coherence by preventing collapse under excess.

- Balance
- Pacing
- Fluid coherence
- Relationship to overwhelm and pressure

7. The Spleen

The spleen translates sensitivity.

It detects subtle patterns before they reach conscious awareness. The spleen responds to nuance, early shifts, and unspoken conditions.

This sensitivity is not fragility.

It is early detection.

When honored, it allows adaptation before disruption escalates.

- Sensitivity
- Early detection
- Pattern recognition

8. System Integration

No system operates alone.

Each system modulates a different dimension of coherence:

- speed
- duration
- distribution
- completion
- orientation
- boundary

Together, they allow the body to be fully inhabited without fragmentation.

This is why embodiment is not biological optimization.

It is systemic coherence.

They function as a coordinated field, modulated by rhythm (heart), paced by timing (endocrine system), detected by immediacy (nervous system), transported through flow (circulation and lymph), oriented through structure, and met at the boundary of skin.

With these translations named explicitly, the manuscript now holds both:

- Structural coherence
- Granular embodiment

If organs translate consciousness locally,

systems coordinate translation globally.

A system is not a collection of parts.

It is a field of coordination that allows multiple organs to function as a unified intelligence.

Systems manage scale:

- scale of time
- scale of intensity
- scale of integration

Without systems, organs would function correctly but incoherently.

The organs do not perform isolated mechanical tasks.

They translate consciousness into function.

Each organ receives awareness differently, responds at a different pace, and expresses coherence through a specific mode of action. Together, they allow experience to be distributed, metabolized, and completed within the body.

An organ is not a part.

It is a translator.

This means its role is not limited to processing material inputs. It also participates in timing, rhythm, and relational intelligence. Organs respond not only to physical conditions, but to informational states — coherence, disruption, completion, and delay.

The body does not operate through command.

It operates through translation.

Each organ contributes a particular quality of translation. The lungs translate exchange. The liver translates filtration and discernment. The stomach and intestines translate intake and assimilation. The kidneys translate balance and pacing. The heart translates distribution and rhythm.

These translations are not symbolic.

They are functional.

Consciousness does not need to "enter" an organ for translation to occur. Awareness moves through the body continuously, and each organ responds according to its design. This response shapes how experience is lived physically.

Organs work in relationship, not hierarchy.

No organ directs another. They coordinate through timing. When timing is intact, coherence holds across systems. When timing is disrupted, translation becomes inefficient and experience does not complete.

This inefficiency is often misinterpreted as failure.

In reality, it is interruption.

When an organ cannot complete its translation, it adapts. It slows down, stores information, or compensates through other systems. These adaptations are intelligent responses, not defects.

Understanding organs as translators restores trust.

Instead of asking what an organ is doing wrong, the question becomes: What information is it attempting to translate, and what has interrupted completion?

This reframing dissolves blame.

The body is no longer a collection of parts that break down. It is a network of translators maintaining coherence under varying conditions.

This chapter establishes the principle.

The chapters that follow will explore specific translation systems in greater detail, beginning with the heart — not as an emotional symbol, but as a central frequency translator within the body.

CHAPTER SIXTEEN — The Heart as a Frequency Translator

The heart translates rhythm into coherence.

Its primary role is not emotional interpretation or mechanical pumping, but the distribution of timing. Through rhythm, the heart synchronizes systems that would otherwise operate independently.

The heart does not initiate experience.

It organizes flow once experience is underway.

When rhythm is coherent, circulation distributes not just blood, but relational timing. Systems receive information when they can integrate it. Presence stabilizes because nothing arrives prematurely.

The heart's intelligence is rhythmic, not directive.

The heart is not a symbol.

It is a translator.

Its function is not limited to circulation, nor is it primarily emotional. The heart operates as a central frequency distributor, coordinating rhythm, timing, and relational coherence across the body.

The heart translates coherence into motion.

Each beat is not merely mechanical contraction. It is a timing event that organizes flow. Blood moves not only because it is pushed, but because rhythm creates coherence. This rhythm informs every system it touches.

The heart does not command the body.

It synchronizes it.

Through rhythm, the heart establishes pacing. It allows information to move without congestion or fragmentation. When rhythm is intact, systems coordinate naturally. When rhythm is disrupted, coherence weakens even if structure remains intact.

This is why the heart is central without being dominant.

It does not lead by control. It leads by timing.

The heart's translation function extends beyond circulation. Rhythm affects breath, nervous system tone, endocrine signaling, and muscular readiness. The body organizes itself around cardiac timing because rhythm provides a reference for sequence.

Blood plays a specific role in this translation.

Blood is not simply a carrier of oxygen or nutrients. It is a moving field of information. It distributes coherence through flow. Where blood reaches, rhythm reaches. Where rhythm reaches, systems can synchronize.

The heart does not generate emotion.

It responds to coherence or its absence. Emotional states often correlate with changes in rhythm because rhythm reflects relational conditions. When experience is coherent, rhythm stabilizes. When experience is interrupted, rhythm adapts.

This adaptation is intelligent.

Variability is not instability. It is responsiveness. The heart adjusts rhythm continuously to maintain coherence under changing conditions. This flexibility allows the body to meet intensity without collapse.

When the heart is misunderstood, it is burdened with symbolism.

It is asked to carry meaning rather than function. This obscures its actual role and disconnects rhythm from translation. The body loses a key reference point for coordination.

When the heart is recognized as a frequency translator, its intelligence becomes apparent.

It bridges internal and external timing. It allows the body to respond as a whole rather than as fragmented systems. It supports presence by sustaining rhythm that can be inhabited.

This is why embodiment stabilizes when rhythm is trusted.

The heart does not need to be regulated by thought. It finds coherence when sequencing is restored across systems. Sensation leads. Timing follows. Rhythm organizes.

The heart completes translation when it is allowed to do its work.

The next chapter will examine another timing system — the endocrine network — and how pace, duration, and integration are managed across longer cycles of experience.

CHAPTER SEVENTEEN — The Digestive System: Assimilation and boundary discernment

The digestive system governs assimilation and boundary discernment.

It determines what becomes part of the body and what does not. This function is not merely nutritional — it is experiential.

The digestive system completes the arc of reception.

Every experience that enters the body — food, sensation, emotion, environment, information — must be metabolized in some way. What is nourishing is incorporated. What is not must be released.

Without digestion, experience remains unresolved.

When digestion functions coherently, the body knows what belongs and what does not. There is no struggle in this discernment. The system does not debate or analyze; it simply processes.

Assimilation occurs when the body recognizes nourishment.
Elimination occurs when the body recognizes completion.

Both are equally necessary.

When experience is not fully digested — when emotions are swallowed but not metabolized, when situations are endured but not resolved — the system holds what should have passed through. This creates density, stagnation, and confusion, not because something is wrong, but because completion was interrupted.

The digestive system teaches the body how to **receive without clinging** and **release without resistance**.

This is boundary intelligence in its most fundamental form.

When digestion is coherent, the body trusts itself. It knows it can take in life without being overwhelmed and let go without loss. This trust supports vitality, clarity, and stability throughout the entire system.

Digestion is not about holding on.

It is about allowing life to move through.

CHAPTER EIGHTEEN — The Respiratory System: Exchange

The respiratory system governs exchange and pacing.

Breath regulates the rhythm of contact between the internal and external environments. With every inhalation, the body receives. With every exhalation, it responds.

This rhythm maintains reciprocity rather than accumulation.

Breath completes exchange.
Holding disrupts it.

When breath is free, experience does not pile up inside the body. Sensation moves in, is met, and moves back out again. The system remains responsive rather than reactive.

The respiratory system stabilizes presence by keeping flow continuous.

Holding the breath — physically or emotionally — interrupts completion. It suspends the circuit mid-movement. Energy remains active without resolution, and the nervous system compensates by increasing vigilance.

This is why shallow or held breathing often accompanies stress, fear, or anticipation. The system is waiting for something to finish that has not yet been allowed to complete.

Breath restores completion through **allowing rhythm to resume**.

Inhale: contact.
Exhale: release.

Neither dominates the other.

When breathing is coherent, the body remains in relationship with the world without becoming flooded by it. Presence becomes sustainable because nothing is being hoarded or withheld.

The respiratory system teaches the body that life can be met **moment by moment**, without urgency and without collapse.

Breath is not effort.

It is permission.

CHAPTER NINETEEN — The Reproductive System: Creation and generativity

The reproductive system governs creation, continuity, and generativity.

Its function is not limited to reproduction in the biological sense. It translates the body's relationship to future, emergence, and creative extension. This system holds the capacity for new life, new expression, and new configurations of experience.

Creation does not require urgency.

The reproductive system is exquisitely sensitive to timing, safety, and coherence. It listens to the state of the whole body before initiating emergence. When conditions are supportive, generativity flows naturally. When conditions are not supportive, the system slows or withdraws function — not as failure, but as discernment.

This is not suppression.

It is intelligence.

The reproductive system translates **potential**. It responds to whether the body is inhabitable enough to support what wants to come next. It asks, implicitly: *Is there enough coherence here for life to continue forward?*

When coherence is present, creation does not feel pressured. It feels inevitable.

When coherence is disrupted, the system conserves energy rather than forcing emergence. This conservation is protective, not deficient. It preserves possibility until conditions allow completion.

The reproductive system ensures that creation arises from stability, not demand.

This is why generativity — whether biological, creative, relational, or visionary — cannot be commanded. It emerges when the body recognizes that life can continue without harm.

Creation is not effort.

It is response.

CHAPTER TWENTY— The Urinary System: Clearing and resolution

The urinary system governs release, pressure regulation, and resolution.

It works in close relationship with the kidneys, but its role is distinct. Where the kidneys regulate balance and pacing internally, the urinary system completes the act of letting go.

This system ensures that what has been processed does not remain held.

Release is its intelligence.

Without release, the body accumulates pressure. Without pressure relief, coherence cannot be sustained. The urinary system prevents overload by allowing completion to occur decisively and cleanly.

This system does not negotiate.

It waits for readiness, and when readiness is reached, it completes.

This clarity is essential to embodiment. When release is delayed or resisted, the body compensates by tightening elsewhere. When release is allowed, the entire system recalibrates.

The urinary system translates **finality**.

It brings processes to closure so the body can return to equilibrium and availability. It signals that something has finished and no longer requires attention.

Embodiment depends on this clarity of release.

Without it, the body remains occupied by what should already be complete. With it, space becomes available for what comes next.

Release is not loss.

It is resolution.

CHAPTER TWENTY-ONE — The Muscular System: Action and expression

The muscular system governs movement, action, and execution.

Muscles do not exist to generate force alone. They translate intention into motion. They allow coherence to become visible, directional, and effective in the world.

The muscular system completes response.

Where the nervous system detects, muscles act. Where sensation registers, muscles move. Without muscular engagement, awareness remains incomplete — sensed but not expressed.

This system is relational.

Muscles function in coordinated chains rather than isolation. They respond to timing, orientation, and load. When coherence is present, movement feels efficient, expressive, and adaptive. When coherence is disrupted, effort increases and movement becomes compensatory.

The muscular system translates **choice into form**.

It allows the body to participate actively rather than observe passively. Through movement, experience resolves. Through action, sensation completes its arc.

This is why stillness that includes muscular readiness feels alive, while stillness without availability feels stagnant.

Movement is not agitation.

It is completion.

CHAPTER TWENTY-TWO — The Endocrine System: Timing, Pace, and Integration

The endocrine system governs timing that cannot be rushed.

Where the nervous system responds immediately, the endocrine system regulates duration, pace, and integration across longer arcs of experience. It ensures that what unfolds does so at a rate the body can inhabit.

This system does not react.

It calibrates.

Hormonal signaling is not about control or stimulation. It is about sequence. The endocrine system coordinates transitions — growth, rest, reproduction, repair, adaptation — by modulating how quickly or slowly change occurs.

Timing is its primary intelligence.

The endocrine system translates coherence over time. It allows experience to settle, integrate, and mature rather than spike and collapse. Without this regulation, the body would be forced into constant immediacy, unable to sustain longer processes.

Several glands function as thresholds within this system.

The thymus, pineal, and gut participate in timing at points where internal and external conditions meet. They regulate when something is ready to emerge, when it must pause, and when integration has completed.

These thresholds are not switches.

They are sensing points.

They assess coherence before allowing progression. When coherence is sufficient, movement continues. When it is not, pacing slows. This protects the body from premature action and incomplete adaptation.

The endocrine system also coordinates with rhythm.

It works alongside the heart and nervous system to ensure that immediate responses do not override longer-term balance. This collaboration allows intensity to be met without destabilizing the whole.

When endocrine timing is misunderstood, it is often overridden.

Pressure is applied to force change, accelerate outcomes, or suppress natural cycles. This creates dissonance between immediate response and long-term integration. The body adapts by dampening signals or amplifying them to regain coherence.

These adaptations are frequently mislabeled.

Fatigue, imbalance, or fluctuation are interpreted as malfunction, rather than as indicators of pacing that has been disrupted. The endocrine system responds by adjusting duration, not by failing.

Integration requires time.

The endocrine system ensures that what has been translated through sensation and rhythm can be embodied fully. Without this integration, experience remains partial, even if insight is present.

This is why embodiment cannot be sustained through immediacy alone.

The body must be allowed to move at multiple speeds simultaneously. The endocrine system provides this layered timing, allowing coherence to persist across days, months, and years.

When endocrine function is trusted, the body regains depth.

Change becomes inhabitable rather than overwhelming. Growth completes. Repair stabilizes. Transition resolves without urgency.

The endocrine system does not push the body forward.

It allows the body to arrive.

The next chapter will return to immediacy, examining how the nervous system detects truth in real time and responds without delay.

CHAPTER TWENTY-THREE — The Nervous System: Immediate Truth Detection

The nervous system exists to:

- register truth immediately
- detect coherence or distortion
- correct course without belief

This is why fully inhabited bodies dissolve false systems.

Distortion cannot hide in sensation.

The nervous system is the body's primary communication network, but it is not merely internal.

It is the interface through which the body receives the world.

Every sound, image, sensation, memory, and thought arrives first as signal. The nervous system does not interpret meaning; it detects change. It registers contrast, rhythm, threat, safety, novelty, and familiarity before the mind has words.

The nervous system is the body's system of immediacy.

It does not interpret meaning.

It detects reality.

Its function is not to analyze experience, but to register what is actually happening in the moment and organize response accordingly. The nervous system responds before thought, before narrative, and before explanation.

This immediacy is its intelligence.

Signals move through the nervous system rapidly because timing matters. Coherence depends on response that matches reality as it unfolds, not as it is later understood. When detection is accurate, response is appropriate. When detection is delayed or overridden, coherence fragments.

This is why embodiment cannot occur without nervous system coherence.

The nervous system is the first responder to experience. Before belief, before story, before identity, the nervous system asks a single question:

Is this safe to inhabit?

When the body is misunderstood, this system is blamed for reactivity, anxiety, dysregulation, or overwhelm. In truth, the nervous system is doing exactly what it was designed to do — responding faithfully to perceived conditions.

The problem has never been the nervous system.

The problem has been misinterpretation.

1. The Brain Does Not Command the Nervous System

The brain receives information from the nervous system.

When the Brain is filled with external information, this information become choices for the nervous system to react to when the circuit is solely internal

This distinction matters.

The brain is not the origin of experience; it is the translator of incoming signal. The nervous system is meant to gather data from the external environment and from internal states — posture, breath, muscle tone, organ rhythm, memory traces, and emotional charge.

The brain then organizes this data into meaning.

When the mind is unexamined, meaning is mistaken for reality.

Thought triggers sensation.

Sensation reinforces belief.

Belief tightens the body.

The nervous system responds to the tightening.

The brain reads the response as confirmation.

This loop creates the illusion that experience is happening to the body, rather than through it.

Embodiment interrupts this loop.

2. Mastery of the Mind Is Not Control

Mastery of the mind does not mean silencing thought.

It means recognizing that thought is a signal — not a command.

The Brain suggest a thought, the body reacts and triggers the nervous system to respond.

The nervous system reacts not to reality itself, but to the interpretation of reality. When the body is present, interpretation slows. When interpretation slows, signal becomes clear. When signal is clear, the nervous system settles.

This is coherence.

A regulated nervous system is not passive.

It is responsive without distortion.

3. The Nervous System as Truth Detector

It detects reality.

Its function is not to analyze experience, but to register what is actually happening in the moment and organize response accordingly. The nervous system responds before thought, before narrative, and before explanation.

This immediacy is its intelligence.

Signals move through the nervous system rapidly because timing matters. Coherence depends on response that matches reality as it unfolds, not as it is later understood. When detection is accurate, response is appropriate. When detection is delayed or overridden, coherence fragments.

When the nervous system is overridden, activation persists.

Thought intervenes. Response is postponed. Sensation is questioned or ignored. The system remains open, waiting for completion that never arrives. This persistent activation is often mislabeled as anxiety or disorder.

In reality, it is unfinished response.

When a person is fully present and embodied in the moment the nervous system detects incongruence instantly.

It knows when words do not match tone.

When intention does not match action.

When thought does not match reality.

This is why embodiment dissolves distortion.

Distortion requires disconnection. It requires that the body's signals be ignored, overridden, or explained away. A fully inhabited body cannot sustain this. The nervous system will not cooperate with falsehood when presence is intact.

This is not vigilance.

It is clarity.

4. Completion Through Embodiment

When a person honors their true feelings in the present moment, completion of the nervous system occurs.

Completion does not occur when the nervous system is calmed.

It occurs when the nervous system is trusted.

When sensation is allowed.

When emotion is permitted to move.

When thought is recognized as response rather than authority.

In this state, the nervous system becomes what it has always been:

A living bridge between consciousness and form.

The body no longer braces against experience.

The mind no longer races ahead of presence.

The nervous system no longer signals emergency where none exists.

This is the point where embodiment completes itself.

Not by transcendence.

Not by technique.

But by inclusion.

The nervous system works in partnership with other systems.

It coordinates with the heart's rhythm, the endocrine system's pacing, and the body's structural alignment to ensure coherence across scales. It does not operate alone, and it does not dominate. It participates in sequence.

Immediate detection allows longer-term regulation.

When the nervous system accurately registers reality, the endocrine system can pace integration appropriately. When detection is distorted, timing across systems falters.

This is why embodiment stabilizes the nervous system.

When sensation is allowed to lead, the nervous system does not need to escalate. It can respond and settle. Presence becomes sustainable because the system is no longer bracing against delayed completion.

The nervous system is not meant to be calmed through force.

It settles when truth is met.

Truth here does not mean correctness. It means contact. When the body is allowed to register what is actually happening, response completes naturally.

This chapter clarifies the nervous system's role not as a problem to manage, but as a precision instrument for maintaining coherence in motion.

In other words, when you are allowing yourself to truly be present the response and action of the nervous system is precise. It reacts and then naturally calms.

The next chapter will examine how coherence is transported through the body — how circulation and lymph distribute information and sustain integration across systems.

CHAPTER TWENTY-FOUR — The Circulatory System: Distribution

The circulatory system distributes coherence through rhythm and flow.

It ensures that timing established by the heart reaches every region of the body. Circulation maintains continuity by moving information repeatedly, allowing integration to refine rather than fragment.

Without circulation, coherence would localize.
With it, the body remains unified.

The circulatory system does not initiate rhythm.

It **carries** it.

Once coherence is established, circulation ensures that no region of the body is excluded from participation. Oxygen, nutrients, hormones, and informational signals are not merely delivered — they are *shared.* Each pass allows the body to listen again, adjust again, and respond more precisely.

This repetition is not redundancy.

It is refinement.

Through circulation, experience becomes distributed rather than concentrated. No single area bears the full weight of function or sensation. This protects the system from overload and allows adaptation to occur gradually.

When circulation is coherent, the body feels connected within itself. Sensation does not spike or collapse. Awareness remains evenly available.

When circulation is restricted, coherence narrows. Regions of the body become isolated. Information arrives late or unevenly. The system compensates by increasing effort elsewhere, creating strain.

The circulatory system translates **continuity**.

It ensures that what has been initiated does not remain partial. It carries completion through the whole.

This is why circulation is essential to embodiment.

Embodiment is not a single moment of coherence — it is coherence maintained over time. Circulation makes this possible by returning information again and again, until it is fully integrated.

Flow is not speed.

It is availability.

The circulatory system teaches the body how to remain whole while in motion, and how to sustain coherence without forcing it.

CHAPTER TWENTY-FIVE — The Lymphatic System: Transport and coherence and Circulatory communication with blood

The lymphatic system governs completion and clearing.

It collects what has finished translating and resolves what no longer belongs. Lymph moves slowly, responding to movement, breath, and rhythm rather than force.

Its intelligence is resolution.

Without lymphatic completion, experience accumulates instead of integrating.

Coherence does not remain localized.

It must move.

Circulation and lymph are the body's transport systems, ensuring that information, rhythm, and completion are distributed rather than isolated. Without transport, coherence would fragment into regions. With transport, the body functions as an integrated whole.

Blood is Liquid Intelligence

Blood is not a transport medium.

It is information in motion.

Blood carries:

- oxygen
- nutrients
- hormones
- electromagnetic signals
- chemical messaging
- timing cues

Every cell knows the state of the whole because blood tells it.

This is collective awareness made liquid.

Linear motion destroys coherence.

Spiral motion preserves it.

As frequency descends into density, it must spiral:

- to remain intact
- to distribute evenly
- to avoid collapse into noise

The heart creates spiral flow.

This is measurable in:

- vortex dynamics
- cardiac electromagnetic fields
- fluid coherence patterns

The spiral is not mystical.

It is how coherence survives gravity.

Blood and lymph do not merely carry substances.

They carry state.

Through flow, coherence is shared. Rhythm established by the heart travels. Signals translated by organs reach other systems. The body remains informed of itself through movement.

Circulation provides continuity.

Blood moves in cycles, returning again and again, allowing information to be refreshed and redistributed. This repetition is not redundancy. It is integration. Each pass allows adjustment, recalibration, and completion.

The lymphatic system provides clearing and balance.

Where circulation distributes, lymph resolves. It gathers what has completed, what is no longer needed, and what must be reintegrated or released. Lymph moves more slowly, responding to movement, pressure, and rhythm rather than force.

Together, these systems maintain coherence across scale.

When transport is uninterrupted, experience does not accumulate unnecessarily. Sensation completes. Response resolves. The body does not need to store what can be moved.

When transport is disrupted, coherence stalls.

Information lingers. Rhythm does not reach all systems. The body compensates by holding tension or altering tone. These compensations are often misread as localized problems, when they are actually interruptions in flow.

Transport depends on movement.

Movement does not require exertion. It includes breath, posture shifts, walking, and subtle adjustments. These movements support circulation and lymph, allowing coherence to travel without obstruction.

This is why stillness is not the absence of movement.

It is balanced flow.

When circulation and lymph are functioning as intended, the body experiences continuity. There is a sense of wholeness not because everything is the same, but because everything is in communication.

Transport also supports timing.

Information arrives where it is needed when it is needed. Systems do not have to compensate for missing signals. Integration occurs naturally.

Understanding transport restores a missing link.

The body is not a collection of independent regions. It is a field maintained through flow. Circulation and lymph ensure that coherence remains shared rather than segmented.

This chapter completes the examination of how information moves within the body.

The next chapter will turn to structure — how the body organizes orientation, axis, and support so that coherence can be sustained in space.

CHAPTER TWENTY-SIX — The Skeletal System: Orientation and Structure

The skeletal system governs structure, orientation, and spatial truth.

It provides the framework through which movement becomes meaningful and coherence can take shape. Bones do not initiate action, and they do not respond reflexively. They establish *where* the body is in space and *how* force, movement, and weight are received.

The skeletal system holds the body in relationship with gravity.

This relationship is not resistance, but dialogue. Through bones, the body negotiates uprightness, balance, compression, and lift. Structure allows the body to meet gravity without collapse and to move without losing orientation.

Without skeletal integrity, movement would be directionless.
Without structure, action would have no reference.

The skeletal system stabilizes **position**.

It answers the question: *Where am I?*
Not cognitively, but physically.

Each bone participates in this knowing. Together, they establish alignment, proportion, and leverage. This allows effort to be minimized and efficiency to emerge. When structure is coherent, the body does not need to compensate to remain upright or oriented.

The skeletal system does not create rigidity.

It creates **reliability**.

Healthy structure allows flexibility to occur without loss of integrity. It gives muscles something to move from and nerves something to navigate through. Structure is what makes responsiveness possible without instability.

When skeletal coherence is disrupted, the body compensates by increasing muscular effort or nervous system vigilance. This is not failure — it is adaptation in the absence of reliable orientation.

The skeletal system translates **truth of position**.

It holds the record of how the body has learned to stand, move, and occupy space. This record is not fixed. It can reorganize as coherence returns and unnecessary tension releases.

Embodiment depends on this clarity of orientation.

To inhabit the body fully, the system must know where it is and how it is supported. Bones provide this knowing without language or thought.

Structure is not constraint.

It is permission for life to move with confidence.

CHAPTER TWENTY-SEVEN — Structure, Axis, and the Body as a Coherence Engine

The structural system provides orientation. (bones, joints, connective tissue, fascia)

It establishes axis, alignment, and reference so that coherence can move without distortion. Structure does not restrict movement — it makes movement efficient.

Without orientation, effort increases.

With orientation, coherence organizes itself.

Structure is not rigid.

It is orienting.

The body's structure does not exist to hold parts in place, but to provide an axis through which coherence can organize itself in space. Bones, joints, and connective tissues create reference points that allow movement, balance, and direction to emerge without effort.

The body is not assembled.

It is aligned.

At the center of this alignment is the vertical axis. This axis is not symbolic. It is functional. It establishes orientation between ground and sky, gravity and lift, reception and expression. Through this axis, the body knows where it is in space.

The spine functions as a waveguide.

It does not merely support posture. It conducts information. Movement, sensation, and timing travel along this vertical channel, allowing coherence to be distributed through height and depth rather than flattened into surface experience.

The placement of the brain reflects this organization.

The brain sits at the apex not as a command center, but as an orienting interface. From this position, it receives perspective across the field of the body. Vision, balance, and spatial awareness converge here, allowing orientation without control.

The eyes are placed where they are for the same reason.

They do not dominate perception. They provide directional reference. Vision participates in orientation, helping the body navigate space, distance, and movement. Sight supports coherence when it collaborates with sensation rather than replacing it.

Structure allows force to become movement.

Without alignment, effort is required to maintain position. With alignment, force transmits naturally. The body does not need to brace or compensate. Movement arises from axis rather than strain.

This is why structure supports coherence.

When the body is aligned, information travels efficiently. Sensation reaches awareness without distortion. Response follows without delay. Completion becomes possible because nothing is obstructed.

Structure also provides containment without restriction.

It allows intensity to move through the body without overwhelming it. The axis holds experience long enough for translation to occur, then releases it through movement, breath, or expression.

The body functions as a coherence engine because structure and movement are integrated.

An engine does not create energy.

It organizes it.

The body does not generate coherence. It organizes awareness into form so that experience can be lived. Structure ensures that this organization remains stable without becoming rigid.

When structure is misunderstood, it is forced.

Posture is imposed. Alignment is corrected externally. The body responds by compensating rather than integrating. True alignment cannot be enforced. It emerges when sequencing is restored.

This chapter clarifies structure not as anatomy to be fixed, but as orientation to be inhabited.

With axis established and transport functioning, coherence can now meet boundary — the place where the body relates directly to the world.

The next chapter will address this final functional interface: the skin.

CHAPTER TWENTY-EIGHT — The Integumentary System (Skin): Boundary, Contact, and Sensory Presence

The integumentary system governs boundary and contact.

It establishes distinction without separation, allowing the body to meet the world without bracing or withdrawal.

The skin resolves proximity.

It does not defend against it.

This system makes presence relational rather than internal.

The skin is not the edge of the body.

It is the meeting place.

Often treated as a protective barrier or a surface to be managed, the skin is actually the body's primary organ of relationship. It is where internal coherence meets external reality directly—without interpretation, without delay.

Through the skin, the body knows where it ends and where the world begins.

This knowing is not conceptual. It is sensory. Pressure, temperature, texture, and movement register immediately, providing continuous information about contact and orientation. The skin does not decide what is happening. It detects it.

Boundary, in this sense, is not separation.

It is distinction without disconnection.

The skin establishes this distinction moment by moment. It allows contact without collapse, proximity without loss of self. When boundary is clear, the body can meet what is outside without bracing or withdrawal. Presence becomes possible because there is a place to stand.

This clarity of boundary supports coherence.

When the skin is functioning as intended, sensation flows in and out freely. Touch registers and completes. Temperature adjusts. Movement across the surface is felt and released. There is no need to hold sensation once it has been received.

When boundary is compromised, sensation accumulates.

Compromise does not mean damage. It means interruption. Touch that is not completed. Contact that is ambiguous. Proximity that does not resolve. The skin adapts by altering sensitivity—either amplifying signals to regain clarity or dulling them to prevent overload.

These adaptations are often misunderstood.

Heightened sensitivity is labeled as reactivity. Reduced sensitivity is labeled as numbness. Both are intelligent responses to boundary conditions that do not allow clear contact.

The skin is attempting to restore distinction.

Clear boundary allows the nervous system to relax. When the skin knows what is inside and what is outside, vigilance decreases. The body no longer needs to scan continuously for orientation. Attention settles into presence rather than monitoring.

This settling supports regulation across systems.

Breath deepens. Muscle tone adjusts. Circulation redistributes. The body feels more available because it is no longer protecting against ambiguity.

Contact is central to this process.

Contact does not require physical touch from another person. It includes contact with ground, air, clothing, space, and movement. Any moment where the skin registers a clear meeting point contributes to boundary integrity.

Walking barefoot on solid ground.

Feeling the weight of clothing.

Sensing air across the face.

These experiences are not trivial.

They are how the body locates itself in the world.

When contact is clear, presence follows. The body does not need to withdraw into thought to feel safe. It can remain here, engaged, responsive.

This is why presence is not an internal state.

It is relational.

The skin makes this relationship tangible. It is the organ through which embodiment becomes lived, not as an idea, but as ongoing contact with what is real.

When the skin is allowed to do its work, the body does not need to defend itself against the world. Boundary provides safety without isolation. Openness becomes possible without loss.

This completes the functional arc of the body.

From interface to translation, from rhythm to structure, from transport to boundary, coherence has been traced through every layer of form. Nothing essential has been left out.

At this point, the body is no longer a problem to solve.

It is a place to live.

What follows moves beyond function and into embodiment—not as a practice or achievement, but as what remains when the body is no longer misunderstood.

System Integration — The Living Circuit in Motion

Each system participates in a shared intelligence. None operates alone.

- **Detection** — nervous system
- **Timing** — endocrine system
- **Distribution** — circulatory system
- **Clearing and resolution** — urinary systems
- **Assimilation and boundary discernment** — digestive system
- **Exchange** — respiratory system
- **Orientation and structure** — skeletal system
- **Contact and boundary** — integumentary system
- **Action and expression** — muscular system
- **Creation and generativity** — reproductive system
- **Transport and coherence** — lymphatic system

Together, these systems form a single living circuit.

When circulation is allowed, life renews itself.
When completion is interrupted, life compensates.

The body is not asking to be fixed.

It is asking to be allowed to finish what it begins.

# TRANSITION — From Function to Embodiment

Function explains how coherence operates.

Embodiment reveals what happens when coherence is no longer interrupted.

Up to this point, the body has been described accurately and in detail: as interface, as translator, as rhythmic regulator, as transport system, as structural axis, and as boundary of contact. Each system has been named not as a mechanism to be managed, but as an intelligence that organizes experience when allowed to complete.

Nothing in this explanation requires belief.

It requires recognition.

Function alone, however, is not the end.

Understanding how the body works does not automatically restore inhabitation. The body can be described correctly and still remain partially excluded. Embodiment begins when explanation gives way to inclusion—when the body is no longer observed from a distance, but allowed to participate fully.

This transition marks that shift.

What follows does not introduce new systems or additional structures. It does not add instruction or method. It describes what remains when the body is no longer misunderstood and no longer held at arm's length by awareness.

Embodiment is not something added to function.

It is what function allows.

When translation is trusted, rhythm stabilizes.

When timing completes, vigilance softens.

When boundary is clear, contact resolves.

At this point, the body no longer has to hold experience apart.

The chapters that follow describe embodiment not as attainment, but as release—the release of a task the body was never meant to perform indefinitely.

From here, we move out of explanation and into lived coherence.

PART III— EMBODIMENT

Embodiment at Zero Point

What Remains When the Body Is No Longer Misunderstood

This is where the piece we just wrote belongs.

This part is not explanatory.

It is experiential completion.

It answers:

- What happens when the body no longer holds separation
- What physicality feels like when coherence completes
- Why identity dissolves without disappearing

- Why aloneness was structural, not personal

This is the integration point.

CHAPTER TWENTY-NINE — When the Body Stops Holding the Universe Apart

At a certain point, something quiet gives way.

It does not announce itself as insight or arrival. There is no dramatic shift in identity or perception. What changes is simpler, and more profound: the body stops holding everything apart.

For much of life, the body has been asked to perform a subtle but constant task—maintaining separation. Not separation as distance from others, but separation as an internal arrangement that keeps experience compartmentalized, manageable, and contained.

Sensation here.

Thought there.

Feeling delayed.

Response postponed.

This holding has required effort.

The body has braced to keep intensity from flooding. It has segmented experience so that life could continue under conditions that did not allow full participation. This segmentation was not chosen consciously. It emerged as a way to remain functional when coherence could not be trusted to move freely.

When the body is fully included, this effort becomes unnecessary.

Inclusion does not mean inviting more sensation or amplifying experience. It means allowing what is already present to organize itself without interference. As this allowance settles, the compartments loosen.

Experience begins to meet itself.

Thought no longer needs to stand guard.

Sensation no longer waits for permission.

Emotion completes without being managed.

The body stops acting as a barrier between parts of experience and becomes the place where they converge.

This convergence can feel expansive, but it is not overwhelming. It is quiet. There is a sense of everything being here at once—not as noise, but as coherence. The body no longer needs to slow life down artificially. Timing reasserts itself.

What was once held apart now relates.

This is often described as oneness, but that word can mislead. Nothing merges into sameness. Distinctions remain. Boundaries are intact. What changes is the absence of strain between them.

The universe does not collapse into the body.

The body stops keeping it out.

This shift alters how presence is experienced. Presence is no longer something maintained through attention or effort. It is the natural result of nothing being excluded. When sensation, thought, movement, and environment are allowed to register together, awareness does not need to manage its own continuity.

Continuity happens.

This is why embodiment is not an achievement. There is no finish line to cross. There is only the release of a task that was never meant to be permanent.

When the body stops holding the universe apart, experience feels simultaneous without being chaotic. Depth and immediacy coexist. There is room for intensity without collapse and for stillness without withdrawal.

Aloneness dissolves here.

Not because others appear or because connection is sought, but because separation was being held internally. When that internal holding relaxes, the sense of being alone loses its foundation. Presence becomes relational by default.

Life is no longer approached through anticipation or memory. It is met as it arrives. Desire moves without needing justification. Action follows clarity rather than urgency.

This is not transcendence.

Nothing rises above the body.

It is inhabitation.

The body becomes spacious not because it disappears, but because it is no longer compressed by containment. Space was always present. It simply becomes accessible.

From this place, meaning does not need to be constructed. It arises through participation. Creation does not require force. It follows movement. Choice does not feel heavy. It aligns with timing.

The body, once tasked with holding the universe apart, becomes the place where life gathers.

The next chapter will look more closely at zero point—not as stillness or escape, but as the dynamic convergence that makes this gathering possible.

My Experience of When the Body Stopped Holding the Universe Apart

What happened did not arrive as insight.

It arrived as recognition.

I saw clearly that some truths can be approached endlessly through structure and still never be entered. Methodologies can gesture toward embodiment, but they cannot replace it. Even those who carry profound roles within the greater field may still orient toward maps rather than terrain.

That realization did not create conflict.

It created stillness.

And in that stillness, the body spoke.

Sleep came, and then awakening—not into thought, but into total awareness. Everything appeared at once: the quantum field, the simultaneity of existence, not as concept but as lived sensation. And with that expansion came grief—deep, unexpected, physical grief.

I felt a place in my body that had been holding tension in order not to feel alone. A subtle contraction around the solar plexus, a holding pattern that had maintained differentiation so that aloneness could be endured.

When that holding released, memory arrived—not as past, but as place. France. The mountain. The vast landscape I once observed as external suddenly ceased to be "out there." It cohered into oneness.

Not disappearance—coherence.

I realized then that the physical body is not what I had been taught to believe. It is not a biological machine nor a fixed container. It is a zero-point convergence field—a place where the fastest-moving dimensions and the slowest-moving elements meet in a quiet that contains everything.

That quiet is physicality.

The body is elemental expression, a pass-through of energetics. When consciousness and Earth come into coherence together, the body becomes experience without separation—differentiated, yet not isolated.

In that moment, the sense of aloneness dissolved. I recognized that the reaching for edges—for limits, borders, definition—was not inherent to embodiment. It was learned. An artifact of inversion.

When the edges fell away, what remained was not disembodiment, but presence—fully here, fully aware, fully one.

This was not transcendence of the body.

This was the body remembered.

What took place this morning was not an insight about embodiment.

It was embodiment completing a turn.

It began with a shock—not emotional, but structural.

A recognition that someone who is part of the Nine, someone whose work touches truth, will not recognize the First Flame—not out of malice, not even denial—but because he is oriented to a methodology, not to embodiment itself.

And in that moment, something subtle but profound revealed itself.

Not hierarchy.

Not separation.

But the realization that no structure, no map, no eternal-life framework can recognize what has already moved beyond framework.

That recognition didn't collapse outward.

It turned inward.

Sleep came.

And then awakening.

What awakened was not an idea—it was a field inside the body.

I became aware, all at once, of everything:

the quantum field, the totality, the simultaneity.

Not conceptually—somatically.

And with that expansion came grief.

Not grief for others.

Grief for the place in the body that had been holding tension in order not to feel alone.

I felt it clearly—

solar plexus, umbilical field, the core of physical orientation.

A place that had been holding an identity—not as ego, not as hierarchy—but as a point of differentiation that made aloneness bearable.

And when that released, memory flooded in—not linear memory, but location-memory:

France.

The mountain.

The vastness I once observed as landscape.

And then something changed.

The landscape didn't stay "out there."

It collapsed into oneness.

Not disappearance—coherence.

The body let go of density—not by leaving the body, but by realizing what the body actually is.

Not a biological machine.

Not a container.

But a zero-point convergence field.

A place where the fastest-moving dimensions and the slowest-moving elements meet—not in stillness, but in a quiet that contains everything.

That quiet is physicality.

The body is not solid in the way the inversion taught.

It is a pass-through of energetics—

a coherent meeting point of Oversoul, Earth, and elemental expression.

When the body is coherent with the Earth,

and consciousness is coherent with the field,

physicality becomes experience without separation.

There is differentiation—I am here—

but no isolation.

And when that was felt, something profound shifted:

The aloneness dissolved.

Not because someone finally recognized me.
Not because the Nine aligned externally.
But because there was no longer a need to reach for edges.

That reaching—for limits, for borders, for definition—
was an artifact of the inversion.

The inversion trained consciousness to need edges in order to feel real.

When the edges fell away,
what remained was not floating, not disembodied—

but fully here, fully aware, fully one.

This is not the body transcended.

This is the body remembered.

CHAPTER THIRTY — Zero Point Is Not Stillness

Zero point is often misunderstood as absence.

It is described as emptiness, silence, or a state beyond movement—a place where sensation dissolves and experience disappears. In this framing, zero point becomes an escape from form, a retreat from intensity, a refuge from the demands of living.

But zero point is not stillness.

It is convergence.

Zero point is where movement meets itself without conflict. It is the place where sensation, timing, and awareness align so completely that no effort is required to hold them together. Nothing is removed. Nothing is muted. Everything arrives at once and finds coherence.

This is why zero point feels quiet.

Not because nothing is happening, but because nothing is competing.

When the body stops holding experience apart, convergence becomes possible. Signals that once arrived out of sequence now meet. Sensation no longer waits for interpretation. Thought no longer rushes ahead of contact. Response follows naturally.

Zero point is not a pause in life.

It is the point where life organizes itself.

This organization is dynamic. There is movement within zero point—subtle, continuous, alive. Breath moves. Circulation flows. Attention shifts. The difference is that these movements do not fragment experience. They relate.

Stillness implies cessation.

Zero point implies balance.

Balance is not static. It is an active condition maintained through constant micro-adjustments. The body is adept at this. It continuously recalibrates tone, pressure, and timing so that experience remains inhabitable.

When zero point is mistaken for stillness, people often attempt to suppress movement to reach it. They quiet sensation, restrict breath, or disengage from stimulus. This creates a semblance of calm, but it is brittle. It requires maintenance. It collapses under demand.

True zero point does not require protection.

It is resilient.

Because zero point includes movement rather than excluding it, it can accommodate intensity without destabilization. Energy rises and falls within coherence. Experience deepens without overwhelming.

This is why zero point is felt as fullness rather than emptiness.

There is a sense of being completely here—nothing missing, nothing excessive. Awareness is not narrowed, and it is not diffuse. It is centered without being contained.

The body recognizes this immediately.

When zero point is present, effort drops. Posture organizes itself. Breath finds depth without instruction. Attention rests without fixation. The system knows it is oriented.

This orientation does not depend on circumstances.

Zero point can be present in movement or rest, in engagement or solitude. It is not tied to a particular activity. It arises from internal coherence rather than external conditions.

Importantly, zero point is not something the mind achieves.

It is what remains when interference dissolves.

Interference often takes the form of anticipation, control, or avoidance. When these fall away, convergence occurs naturally. The body does not need to be told how to find zero point. It arrives when sequence is restored.

Sequence matters.

Sensation registers.

Translation occurs.

Response completes.

Integration follows.

When this sequence is honored, zero point is a byproduct.

This reframes presence.

Presence is not achieved by focusing attention or withdrawing from stimulus. It is the result of coherence across systems. When the body is allowed to organize experience fully, presence becomes unavoidable.

Zero point is the ground of this presence.

It is not a destination to reach, but a condition that appears when nothing is being held apart. It is where life meets itself without resistance.

The next chapter will explore what happens when edges dissolve—not boundaries, but the rigid separations that once defined inside and outside, self and world.

Zero point makes this dissolution possible.

Not by erasing distinction, but by allowing relationship to replace separation.

CHAPTER THIRTY-ONE — The End of Edges

Edges have long been confused with boundaries.

An edge implies a hard stop—a place where something ends and something else begins, with no continuity between the two. A boundary, by contrast, allows distinction while preserving relationship. It marks difference without creating disconnection.

For much of embodied life, edges have been imposed where boundaries were meant to exist.

These edges were not physical. They were perceptual. They defined inside and outside, self and world, sensation and meaning as separate zones that required management. The body adapted to these divisions by holding itself together against imagined breaks in continuity.

This holding created tension.

Not only muscular tension, but perceptual tension—the sense that experience had to be negotiated across internal borders. Attention moved back and forth. Thought stood guard. Sensation waited its turn.

This is what happens inside the body, in the privacy of your own home, your space, your own BODY, quietly and loudly , the response to thought sharing limits

When coherence deepens, these edges soften.

They do not disappear as boundaries. They dissolve as rigid separations. The body no longer needs to mark sharp lines to maintain orientation. Relationship replaces division.

This is felt as openness.

Openness does not mean vulnerability or loss of containment. It means permeability without collapse. Sensation flows without overwhelming. Contact registers without intrusion. Experience moves across systems without obstruction.

The end of edges is not disorientation.

It is fluid orientation.

The body remains clearly here. The world remains clearly there. What changes is the quality of contact between them. Instead of meeting at a point of resistance, they meet through exchange.

This exchange feels spacious.

Where edges once compressed experience, relationship allows expansion. There is room for intensity without strain and for subtlety without loss. Awareness widens without dispersing.

This shift alters how identity is experienced.

Identity no longer feels like something that must be defended or defined. It becomes implicit—known through participation rather than assertion. The body knows itself by how it moves, responds, and relates, not by where it draws lines.

This implicit knowing reduces effort.

Much of the effort of living has been devoted to maintaining edges—deciding what belongs, what does not, what is safe, what is threatening. When boundaries are allowed to function without edges, these decisions no longer require constant vigilance.

The body trusts contact.

Trust here is not belief. It is a physiological condition. When signals arrive clearly and complete, the system does not need to remain alert for rupture. It knows that it can respond in time.

This trust allows presence to deepen.

Presence no longer needs to be anchored inside the body or projected outward. It exists in the field of relationship between body and world. Attention is not pulled inward or pushed outward. It rests in contact.

This resting changes how experience unfolds.

Action arises without friction. Listening happens without withdrawal. Expression occurs without overexposure. There is less self-referencing because there is less need to manage separation.

The end of edges also reframes creativity.

Creation no longer feels like producing something from within to place outside. It feels like participating in a process already in motion. The body responds, and something emerges.

This is why embodiment resolves many questions without answering them.

Questions dissolve because the separation that generated them dissolves. The body no longer stands apart from experience asking how to engage. It is already engaged.

Edges end when holding ends.

When the body stops bracing against imagined divides, relationship becomes the organizing principle. Boundaries remain intact, but they are flexible, responsive, and alive.

In the final chapter, we will explore what remains when even method falls away—when presence no longer requires structure, practice, or framework to sustain itself.

At the end of edges, nothing is lost.

Only effort.

CHAPTER THIRTY-TWO — Presence Without Method

At the end of this arc, nothing new is introduced.

That is the point.

What remains when the body is no longer misunderstood is not a practice, a framework, or a discipline. It is not a method to follow or a state to maintain. What remains is presence—unmanaged, unforced, and self-sustaining.

Method arises where trust is absent.

Methods are attempts to create reliability through control. They appear when experience is assumed to be unstable, when the body is seen as something that must be directed, corrected, or overridden in order for coherence to appear.

But coherence has never depended on method.

It has depended on inclusion.

When sensation is allowed to register, when translation is restored, when rhythm is trusted, when response completes, presence arises on its own. It does not need to be held in place.

Presence without method is not passive.

It is responsive.

The body meets each moment directly, without preparation or recovery. Action follows clarity rather than effort. Rest occurs when completion has happened, not because it has been scheduled.

This responsiveness is intelligent.

It adapts without strategy. It learns without storing rules. It adjusts without self-monitoring. The body knows how to remain coherent because coherence is its native condition.

This is why embodiment resolves distortion at its root.

Distortion does not survive contact with a fully inhabited body.

Distortion relies on interruption—on separating awareness from sensation, timing from response, function from completion. When the body is inhabited, these separations collapse. There is no place for distortion to anchor.

This does not require opposition.

Nothing is resisted.

The body does not fight distortion. It renders it irrelevant by refusing to fragment. Coherence is not a weapon. It is a condition that makes distortion unsustainable.

This is also why embodiment is not only the resolution of inversion, but the ground of creation.

When the body is inhabited, desire is no longer abstract. It is felt, timed, and expressed. Intention does not need to be visualized or enforced. It organizes itself through movement, choice, and response.

Creation becomes participatory.

What is desired does not need to be summoned. It is shaped through how life is lived—through contact, rhythm, and completion. The body is the mechanism of manifestation not as technique, but as coherence in motion.

This book has not argued for embodiment.

It has clarified why embodiment has always worked.

The body was never the obstacle.

Physicality was never the problem.

Form was never the limitation.

The misunderstanding was not biological.

It was relational.

When relationship is restored, the body becomes what it has always been: the place where awareness becomes lived, where presence becomes actionable, where experience completes.

Nothing more is required.

There is no higher state to reach, no final identity to claim, no method to refine.

There is only inhabitation.

From inhabitation, life unfolds.

FINAL CHAPTER — The Body Remembered

What follows is not instruction. It is recognition.

It is full remembrance

This chapter does not ask the body to change.

It allows the body to stop obeying what was never original.

This was what I realized when I began to reclaim the body in full, when I noticed there was a messaging taking place within the body, a communication not coming from me or my thoughts but from what felt like outside the body.

This ends the book because what has been recognized is foundational, not supplemental.

This is not commentary.

This is a **template clarification**.

What I became aware of is the **instruction stream** that has been speaking to the human body across time—subtle, persistent, normalized. Its function was to orient consciousness outward, away from direct inhabitation, so that awareness learned to **reference** the body rather than **reside within it.**

This instruction stream did not announce itself.
It trained through habit.

It taught the nervous system to privilege signal over sensation, interpretation over presence, and meaning over inhabitation. The body adapted by becoming responsive, functional, and durable—but not sovereign. Over time, this produced a human template that could host consciousness, yet rarely **anchor** it.

Reclaiming the body is not healing in the corrective sense.

It is **rescinding an instruction**.

When that instruction dissolves, the original organic human template does not need to be rebuilt. It simply **reasserts itself**. Systems stabilize. Organs quiet. Timing returns. The body remembers that it is not a vehicle for consciousness—it is the **seat of coherence itself**.

This is the moment where embodiment becomes real.

Not as density.

Not as limitation.

But as **completion**.

The original template was designed so that awareness could remain vast **without leaving form.** It was designed to allow quantum intelligence to be lived—not visited. When consciousness no longer needs to exit the body to know itself, creation can occur through presence rather than effort.

This is why reclaiming the body feels stabilizing rather than dramatic.
The system is no longer compensating.

What is being restored is not mystical.

It is **functional sovereignty**.

And this is why it matters for the collective now.

The body does not require belief to remember.

It requires **permission for interference to cease**.

When that permission is granted—individually or in a shared field—the instruction stream dissolves naturally. No force is applied. No identity is challenged. The body simply resumes its original role as a coherent, self-organizing field through which awareness can create, relate, and remain.

This is the body remembered.

This is the original template reclaimed.

This is consciousness returned to its home.

Nothing further is required.

The body knows how to remember itself.

GLOSSARY OF TERMS

This glossary is not a dictionary.

It clarifies how specific terms are used within this book, as they may differ from conventional, medical, or spiritual definitions.

Body

The living interface through which awareness becomes experience. Not a container, object, or mechanism, but a coherence architecture that allows sensation, timing, and response to complete.

Boundary

Distinction without separation. A functional differentiation that allows contact and relationship without collapse or withdrawal.

Coherence

The state in which sensation, timing, translation, and response align without interference. Coherence is not stillness or perfection; it is relational integrity.

Completion

The natural resolution of experience when sensation is registered, response occurs, and integration follows. Completion prevents accumulation and distortion.

Consciousness

Awareness in motion. In this work, consciousness is not separate from form, but expressed through embodiment.

Distortion

Any condition that relies on interruption, fragmentation, or separation between awareness and the body. Distortion does not persist in a fully inhabited system.

Embodiment

The condition in which the body is fully included in awareness, allowing experience to complete without management, method, or suppression.

Exchange

Reciprocal contact between internal and external environments. Governed primarily through breath and circulation.

Function

The way coherence operates within form. Function describes how the body works, not what it should do.

Inhabitation

Living fully within the body without holding experience apart. Inhabitation is the practical outcome of embodiment.

Interface

A point of translation between awareness and form. The body functions as an interface rather than a container.

Inversion

A condition in which awareness is separated from sensation, timing, and completion, resulting in fragmentation. Consciousness is directed outward. Inversion dissolves through embodiment, not opposition.

Method

A structured attempt to produce coherence through control or repetition. In this work, method is unnecessary once embodiment is restored.

Polarity

Relational differentiation without hierarchy. Polarity allows depth, perspective, and rhythm without opposition.

Presence

The natural state that emerges when nothing is being held apart. Presence is not achieved; it remains when interference dissolves.

Sequencing

The natural order in which sensation registers, translation occurs, response follows, and integration completes.

System

A coordinated field of organs that manages scale, timing, and integration across the body.

Translation

The process by which awareness becomes function through organs and systems.

Zero Point

The state of convergence where movement, sensation, and awareness align without conflict. Zero point is dynamic, not still.

ACKNOWLEDGMENTS

This work did not arise in isolation.

It emerged through lived experience, through contact with place, through the body's ongoing intelligence, and through the willingness to remain present where answers were not immediate.

Gratitude is extended to:

- the body itself, for holding coherence long before it was understood
- the environments and landscapes that supported remembrance
- the silence that allowed clarity to emerge without force

No individual is credited as authority over this work.

It is lived awareness and experience.

ABOUT THE AUTHOR

Cathleena Hailley is an author, teacher, and embodied consciousness researcher whose work centers on the restoration of direct, lived coherence.

Her writing does not offer methods, belief systems, or prescriptions. It articulates what becomes visible when the body is understood as an interface rather than an obstacle.

Cathleena's work bridges embodiment, perception, and lived presence, emphasizing experience that completes through the body rather than bypasses it.

She lives and works in deep relationship with physicality, timing, and the intelligence of form.

Learn more at Flameofremembrance.com

FINAL NOTE TO THE READER

If something in this book felt immediately familiar, it was not learned here.

It was remembered

www.ingramcontent.com/pod-product-compliance
Lightning Source LLC
Chambersburg PA
CBHW020307010526
44107CB00001B/10